Striking Home

Striking Home

*Interpreting and Proclaiming
the New Testament*

Nigel M. Watson

EPWORTH PRESS

British Library Cataloguing in Publication Data

Watson, Nigel M.
Striking home: interpreting and
proclaiming the New Testament.
1. Bible. N.T.——Homiletical use
2. Preaching
I. Title
251   BV4211.2

ISBN 0-7162-0438-X

First published 1987
by Epworth Press
Room 195, Central Buildings,
Westminster, London SW1

Typeset at the Spartan Press Ltd
and printed in Great Britain by
Richard Clay Ltd, Bungay, Suffolk.

To Stella

Contents

Preface

This book has been written in the conviction that the books of the Bible, and of the New Testament in particular, were a word that struck home in their own time and place, and that the task of the preacher is, through disciplined exegesis, so to let them be heard anew that they may strike home once again.

Many of the ideas which have come to fruition in this book were first implanted during two periods of study leave: a semester in Münster in 1980 with Professor Willi Marxsen and another in Zurich in 1986 with Professor Hans Weder. During 1986 I was also able to consult with scholars in Göttingen, Heidelberg, Münster and Tübingen, thanks to a grant from the Deutscher Akademischer Austauschdienst. I also gladly acknowledge the encouragement of my family and of many students, past and present. At its meeting on 15 September 1970, the Ormond College Theological Students' Society was generous enough to pass a motion urging me to consider writing a book along these lines. There are, no doubt, many reasons why it has taken me so long to respond to their request. I hope that not the least reason has been my respect for the importance of the task.

Ormond College,   Nigel M. Watson
Melbourne

1

Introduction

In writing this book, I have had two main aims in mind. The first is to initiate readers into the art of biblical exegesis and, more particularly, the art of New Testament exegesis.

The second is to stimulate reflection on how to make the transition from exegesis to preaching. The first of these aims is pursued in Chapters 1–5 of this book, the second in Chapters 6 and 7. The earlier chapters are therefore more obviously relevant to the concerns of theological students, the later ones to the concerns of parish clergy. It is my hope, however, that students will not put the book down at the end of Chapter 5 and, equally, that parish clergy will not confine their attention to Chapters 6 and 7.

Why Another?

In launching on to the market what is, in part, an introduction to biblical exegesis, I am well aware that there are already several introductory handbooks in the field. In my judgment, however, such handbooks tend to suffer from two serious limitations. First, the exegetical procedures which they propose are often so detailed and complex as to leave the reader feeling quite overwhelmed. Gordon Fee,[1] for example, lists thirty-one steps, while Douglas Stuart has a list of twelve sections with forty-nine sub-sections.[2] Recognizing that parish clergy do not have the time to follow such a detailed procedure, Fee and Stuart both offer, in addition, short guides to exegesis for sermon preparation, but even these are still of a daunting length. Stuart's, for example, contains six headings, comprising twenty-three steps. Stuart's own estimate of the time it would take to work through these steps, which are all preliminary to the preparation of the actual sermon, is five hours. Richard Soulen, in the latest edition of his *Hand-Book of Biblical Criticism* includes in an appendix 'a Simplified Guide for writing an Exegetical Paper on the Synoptic Gospels employing Historical Critical Methods'.[3] This comprises twenty-five steps.

In stressing the complexity of these various outlines, I in no way wish to suggest that any one of these scholars is guilty of pedantic fussiness. Every one of the steps they propose can be given a scholarly rationale. My concern is the effect such outlines have not only on the student beginning his or her biblical studies but also on those parish clergy who want their preaching to be based on solid biblical study but do not have the time to work through twenty-three or twenty-five preliminary steps.

The other weakness I have sometimes observed in exegetical handbooks is a tendency to be long on advice but short on illustrations. It is my conviction, based on more than twenty years of teaching in a theological college, that students will see the point far more quickly if one can produce an example from the Bible to illustrate every assertion one makes. In the chapters which follow, I have tried not to put forward a single proposition without citing at least one biblical passage which illustrates the point.

Authorial Intention?

In formulating a procedure for exegesis, I have had to take up positions on matters which are at the present time the subject of vigorous controversy. Exegetical principles which have been accepted by biblical scholars as axiomatic ever since the Enlightenment are now being challenged. In particular, it has been assumed as a matter of course by generations of biblical scholars that the primary aim of exegesis is to ascertain the intention of the original author. That can no longer be taken for granted, nor (I hope) have I done so. I remain convinced, however, that the determination of the author's intention ought to be seen as the primary aim of the exegesis of New Testament texts and I have tried to justify that position, while recognizing that it is not an aim that we can always be confident of attaining and that the meaning of the text is too rich to be defined in terms of authorial intention alone.

Why Sermons?

In making the transition from exegesis to preaching, we enter another field which is the subject of vigorous contemporary debate. Here too positions which have been accepted by preachers as axiomatic for generations are under challenge and have been so for decades. It can no longer be assumed as a matter of course that the preaching of the Word ought to continue to have the central place in our worship which it has had, in Protestant churches at least, ever since the Reformation. My belief, which I have sought to substantiate, is that preaching ought to continue to have that central place, but I am also convinced that it needs to be far more directly related to the specific situation of our hearers than it often is and I also believe that it needs to be supplemented.

One way among Others

As for the transition from text to sermon, I am particularly interested in one way of making that transition, one which seeks to do justice to what I would call the conspicuously intentional character of the biblical writings, particularly the writings of the New Testament, but I do not believe it is the only valid way or always the most appropriate way.

In defining my second main aim in the opening paragraph of this introduction, I was careful not to say that I was seeking to show the reader how to make the transition from exegesis to preaching but rather to stimulate reflection on how that transition might best be made. The method I am particularly advocating should be regarded as but one way of doing so, but I still believe it is a good way. If what I have written contributes in any way to more disciplined exegesis and the renewal of preaching, I shall be satisfied.

A final footnote: The longer I have worked on this task, the more uneasy I have become about the consistent use of the masculine pronouns, 'him' and 'his' to refer to God, but I cannot think of an entirely satisfactory alternative. To oscillate between 'him' and 'her' is surely confusing, while to substitute 'God' and 'God's' for 'him' and 'his' leads to stylistic infelicities. In the end I have decided to stick to traditional usage.

2

The Intention and the Words

The aim of exegesis has traditionally been understood as being to grasp as clearly as possible the meaning which the original author intended to communicate to the readers he had in view. Understood in this way exegesis is different from paraphrase. Nor should it be confused with a discussion of the historicity of the passage.

This concept of the goal of exegesis is, however, under attack from several sides at once, and in order to resolve the problem I propose the following:

(*a*) The sense of constraint to respect authorial intention, which most interpreters acknowledge, is ethical in nature; (*b*) the obligation to respect authorial intention in dealing with the New Testament texts is inescapable, given their highly personal character; (*c*) any provisional understanding of authorial intention one may have must be rigorously tested by what the author has said and left unsaid; (*d*) the task of ascertaining authorial intention is more or less complex, depending upon which genre one is dealing with; (*e*) it is also complicated by the effective-history of the text in question and by the differences between our life-setting and that of the original readers – these difficulties should not be exaggerated but neither should they be lightly set aside; (*f*) meaning is not exhausted by authorial intention: there are the phenomena of barely conscious motivation and subconscious motivation; there are the levels of meaning which are only disclosed in a new life-setting; there is the inexhaustible richness of all true works of art – all great authors are wiser than they know;

there is the fact that a biblical passage may acquire new levels of meaning or call for some sort of qualification when it is read in the context of the Bible as a whole.

Intention

Students who have written an exegetical exercise sometimes have it returned to them by their assessor with the curt comment, 'All you have done is paraphrase the passage'. Their response is often to say 'But what's wrong with a paraphrase? What else do you expect me to do?'

The short answer to the question, 'What's wrong with a paraphrase?' is that it does not go deep enough. What is expected of you when you write an exegesis on a biblical passage is an effort to get below its surface, so as to be able not simply to restate what the author has written but to offer a coherent interpretation of what he was trying to communicate through what he has written. Exegesis is distinct from paraphrase for the simple reason that intention is distinct from content.

The importance of the distinction between intention and content becomes especially clear in any passage where there is reason to think that the author is using irony, the figure of speech in which (to quote the *Oxford English Dictionary*) 'The intended meaning is the opposite of that expressed by the words used.' If we fail to recognize what is going on in such a passage, the result is bound to be a serious failure of communication. If the penny does eventually drop, we are likely to say to ourselves, in effect, 'How foolish of me to take that literally! Now I see that it was meant ironically.' The same thing is true of passages which employ other literary conventions like parody or allegory or symbolism.

The importance of intention also becomes clearer when one considers the phenomenon of apparent incoherence. Consider, for example, Heb. 13.9–13. Verse 9 is a warning against strange teachings, which includes a disparaging reference to ceremonial foods. Verse 10, however, accepts that we do, after all, have an altar from which those who minister at the tabernacle have no right to eat. Verse 11 then alludes abruptly to what appears to be a ritual of the Day of

Atonement and speaks of the bodies of the victims being burned outside the camp. Verse 12 goes on to speak of Jesus also suffering outside the city gate in order to sanctify his people, while in verse 13 the readers are exhorted to go out to Jesus outside the camp, bearing his disgrace. What exactly is the relationship between the ceremonial foods which are of no value and the altar at which it is a privilege to eat? Or between the burning of sacrificial carcases outside the camp, the suffering of Jesus outside the city gate and the exhortation to go to him outside the camp? As one puzzles over these questions, trying to make sense of the passage as a whole, one inevitably finds oneself asking, 'What led the author to make first this move and then that? What is he trying to communicate through these cryptic and enigmatic statements?' In other words, the search for a coherent meaning compels us to penetrate through the content of the passage to the author's intention.

Readership

A concentration on authorial intention, therefore, is one of the things which set exegesis apart from paraphrase. Another is a concern for readership. Your aim in writing an exegesis is not only to ascertain the author's intention but also to picture as clearly as possible the readers whom the author had in view or at least to picture them as clearly as they were envisaged by the author himself. That qualification is necessary, because the relationship between intention and readership is a complex one. It is no doubt possible for an author to have a firm and clear intention in publishing a book but not have any specific circle of readers in mind. She may be aiming to establish herself as an author. He may be aiming to make as much money as possible. If so, she will have in mind as potential readers anyone who is able to appreciate what she has written. He, on the other hand, will have in mind anyone who can be induced to buy his book. In general, however, there seems to be a positive correlation between intention and readership, in the sense that the clearer an author's intention, the more likely it is that he or she will have in mind a particular circle of readers. Many a would-be

author has had a manuscript rejected by a publisher with the
curt comment, 'It is not clear for whom you are writing or
what you are trying to accomplish.' It will be argued later
that, by and large, the authors of books of the New Testament had not only clear aims in writing but also definite
circles of readers in mind.

Intention and Paraphrase

To illustrate the way in which an exegesis of a passage will
differ from a paraphrase of it, let us consider a particular
passage, the story in John 4.46–54 about the healing of the
son of the royal official. If I were to paraphrase this passage, I
would simply re-tell it in different words. In writing an
exegesis, however, I must grapple above all with these
questions: To what circle of readers is John particularly
addressing himself in telling this story? and, What is he
seeking to communicate to them through it?

My own answer to these questions would be along these
lines: that John is addressing himself particularly to a
community of people who are grieving over the severing of
their last living links with Jesus, people for whom, therefore,
he is in danger of becoming more and more remote, and that
his message for them is that the word of Jesus is a word of
such power that through faith, faith which trusts his word,
faith which trusts without seeing, the life which is his gift
may still be had. No doubt, the details of the interpretation
could and should be debated. What should be clear is that any
exegesis which addresses itself to the questions that we have
proposed is bound to be different from a paraphrase.

The degree of difference, however, will vary depending on
the type of passage one is dealing with, in other words, the
genre. An exegesis of a passage of argument may not differ
very much from a paraphrase of it. That is because a passage
of argument is by its very nature purposive, an attempt to
convince someone of something, 'a connected series of
statements intended to establish a position', to quote a
dictionary definition. Nevertheless an exegesis of a passage
of argument ought to include something which would have
no place in a paraphrase, viz. a reference to the readers to

whom the argument is directed. Thus an exegesis of Gal. 2.16 ought to relate Paul's statement that 'by works of the law shall no one be justified' to the precise situation of the Galatians and the attempt of the Judaizers to get them to accept circumcision. 'To people who are being bullied into believing that in order to be assured of salvation they must be circumcised Paul says. . . .' An exegesis of a passage of argument should differ from mere paraphrase in other ways as well. It should, for example, clarify steps in the argument which the author takes for granted. With narrative or parable, however, the difference between exegesis proper and paraphrase is likely to be more marked. These distinctions of literary form will be explored more thoroughly in the next chapter.

Intentionality and Historicity

In the same way as it is important not to confuse exegesis with paraphrase, so it is important not to confuse the exegesis of a passage of narrative with a discussion of its historicity. As just stated, we shall be giving further attention to the exegesis of narrative in the next chapter. For the present we shall simply state our conviction that biblical narrative has too often been classified with some other mode of discourse, with the result that its uniqueness has not been fully appreciated. Although it is history-like, it is not historical narrative in conformity with the canons of the nineteenth century. Yet at the same time it resists being treated as realistic fiction, an early form of prose realism.[1] The relationship in which it stands to history is not easily defined. On the one hand, the biblical narrators are by no means indifferent to what actually happened. At times they contradict what they regard as mistaken or mischievous accounts of what happened (see e.g. Matt. 28.11–15; John 21.23; Gal. 1.20). And yet the evangelists Matthew and Luke show a remarkable freedom in their use of material from the earlier Gospel, Mark (cf. Matt. 19.17 with Mark 10.18; Luke 24.6f. with Mark 16.7), to say nothing of the use John appears to have made of his sources.

It will help us to see more clearly how far biblical narrative differs from bare chronicle if we turn our attention to a particular narrative, the genealogy in Matthew 1. After listing the ancestors of Jesus, beginning with Abraham, Matthew points out in verse 17 that the period spanned comprises three cycles of fourteen generations: from Abraham to David fourteen generations; and likewise from David to the exile and from the exile to Christ. It is not difficult to see why Matthew found this pattern highly significant. Fourteen is twice seven and seven stands for perfection. Jesus comes at the end of six series of seven generations. He therefore marks the beginning of the seventh series and thus inaugurates the fullness of time. When one compares Matthew's table with the text of the Old Testament, however, one finds that this symmetrical scheme has been arrived at only through the omission of several generations, probably through a hasty reading of the Greek Old Testament. Three kings have dropped out after Uzziah in verse 8 and one king after Josiah in verse 11. Where, then, in this passage does the weight of the meaning lie for Matthew? In the brute fact, if it is a fact (which we have seen reason to doubt), that between Abraham and Jesus three cycles of fourteen generations intervened? Or in the theological truth which he sees expressed in what he believes to have been the pattern of the genealogy linking Abraham and Jesus, the truth that Jesus is the goal of history and the fullness of time? The weight of the meaning for Matthew surely lies in the theological truth.

Some commentators who, if asked, would probably assent to the understanding of exegesis that has been advocated so far allow themselves in practice to be unduly distracted by historical questions. F. W. Beare, for example, in his discussion of Matt. 27.51–53 in *The Earliest Records of Jesus* simply dismisses the events related by Matthew, viz. the earthquake, the splitting of the rocks and the appearance in the holy city of many of the dead, as legendary matter typical of the popular legends that grow around the death of a great man and cites similar stories that arose after the death of Caesar and the passing of the Buddha into Nirvana.[2]

To be sure, the question whether such events as these are historically credible is not unimportant, but it is not the central question of exegesis. The central question for the exegete of a document like St Matthew's Gospel, which is written 'from faith to faith', is rather, 'What truth about God and God's revelation in Jesus Christ is Matthew seeking to communicate through his narrative to his readers?'

To that question Eduard Schweizer does offer an answer, when he writes as follows:

Matthew already reveals glimpses of the victory God has achieved. Not only the darkness but the earthquake, open graves, and dead men walking the streets show that what has taken place here is, in the truest sense of the word, earth-shaking. Death has already been robbed of its power, and the course of the world has been interrupted.[3]

Historical-Critical Exegesis

It would, however, hardly be responsible to uphold the primacy of authorial intention, as we have just done, without also giving some account of the criticisms of the concept which have been made, or are alleged to have been made, over the past sixty years or so, not only in biblical studies but in the wider area of literary criticism. By providing such an account, we shall be able to clarify and substantiate our own position, which is that while authorial intention ought to continue to be regarded as the primary criterion of meaning, at least in dealing with the New Testament, the meaning intended by the original author should not be seen as exhausting the meaning of the passage.

The quest for authorial intention represents the fundamental aim of historical-critical exegesis. It is not difficult to cite a number of books of comparatively recent date in which that understanding of exegesis is accepted without question.[4] To be sure, biblical scholars have readily postulated a process of reinterpretation of the works of biblical authors by subsequent redactors, but each level of redaction can be regarded as representing a form of authorial intention. Furthermore, until the rise of the so-called New Criticism in Britain and America some sixty years ago the quest for the meaning intended by the original author was generally accepted as the fundamental aim of all literary studies. The first question to be asked of any new interpretation being proposed for a literary work was, 'Is this compatible with what the author is likely to have had in mind?'

When first proposed in the eighteenth century, however, by biblical scholars like J. S. Semler and J. Ph. Gabler, the historical-critical method was revolutionary. It was Gabler (1753–1826), in particular, who posed the issue most clearly by his distinction between biblical and dogmatic theology. Biblical theology is, according to Gabler, a purely historical discipline, directed towards establishing the *sensus scriptorum*, that is, what the authors had in mind when they composed the text. As such, it is to be sharply distinguished from dogmatic theology, which subjects the text to historical and philosophical critique.[5] The clarification of these distinctions by scholars like Semler and Gabler and their vindication of historical method in biblical studies were increasingly recognized as a great and liberating achievement, a freeing of the original text from the encrustations of later misconceptions and an assertion of its autonomy over against ecclesiastical tradition. Indeed, the historical-critical method came to be taken for granted as self-evidently correct.

The Historical-Critical Method and its Critics

But all this is true no longer. Historical-critical exegesis is under attack, and from several sides at once. To begin at the beginning, I mention first of all Karl Barth's *Romans* and particularly the preface to the second edition of 1921, in which he protests against recent commentaries on Romans and charges recent commentators with confining themselves to an interpretation of the text which is no commentary at all but merely the first step towards a commentary.[6]

What is it about these commentaries that Barth is protesting against? Some of his pronouncements can be understood as protests against the sort of commentary which limits itself to questions of text and philology and historical parallels rather than to the coherent elucidation of Paul's real intention. Thus he writes that the interpretation of what is written requires 'more than a disjointed series of notes on words and phrases'.[7]

But other statements of Barth's indicate that he is looking for something more than this, viz. a grappling with 'the enigma of the matter', that is, the extrinsic reality to which the text points, until the text seems hardly to exist as a document. 'The Word ought to be exposed in the words.' This is genuine understanding and interpretation, seen at its best in 'that creative energy which Luther exercised with intuitive certainty in his exegesis' and in the work of Calvin, who, 'having first established what stands in the text, sets himself to re-think the whole material and to wrestle with it, till the walls which separate the sixteenth century from the first become transparent! Paul speaks, and the man of the sixteenth century hears'.[8] Clearly, for Barth – and this interpretation is surely borne out by his subsequent writings – only an interpretation on the level of dogmatic theology can do justice to the text.

Bombshell it may have been, yet it is questionable how much effect Barth's *Romans* and subsequent writings have really had on the work of other biblical commentators, either then or in the intervening sixty-five years. Biblical scholars seem to have been more responsive, albeit belatedly, to other currents in the world of scholarship, particularly to secular literary criticism.

The Text Itself

As has already been said, from the Enlightenment until well into this century the quest for the meaning intended by the original author was commonly accepted as the fundamental aim not only of biblical studies but of literary studies generally, but in secular literary criticism this assumption began more and more to be called in question with the rise of New Criticism some sixty years ago. It can even be said that 'there has now come to be a consensus in literary criticism, both in Europe and in the English-speaking world, that a critic's task is to explicate *texts*, not authors'.[9] John Barton, whom I have just quoted, adds that 'the consensus is such that most biblical criticism in the traditional mould, except perhaps for the very latest kinds of redaction criticism, strikes secular critics as fairly out-of-date in style'.[10] Any equation of the meaning of a text with the meaning intended by the original author would be widely seen as a quite

arbitrary restriction of the meaning of 'meaning'. While the
hegemony of New Criticism in British and American uni-
versities is by now a thing of the past, its fundamental
assumptions persist in a great deal of contemporary criticism, however post-New Critical it professes to be.[11] Struc-
turalism, semiotics, narratology, intertextuality, rhetorical
criticism, deconstruction – for all their variations, all these
movements are characterized by a concentration on the text
rather than the author, and on the formal properties of the
text, its texture and structure. Furthermore, they have
begun to have a profound effect on biblical studies also, at
least in certain countries – in France and America a good
deal more than in Britain and Germany, Asia and
Australasia.

Canonical Criticism

Then there is the challenge presented by the advocates of
Canonical Criticism, James A. Sanders and more especially
Brevard Childs. Having already challenged the community
of biblical scholars, but more particularly Old Testament
scholars, with his earlier works: *Biblical Theology in Crisis*
(1970) and *Introduction to the Old Testament as Scripture*
(1979), Professor Childs has now produced an introduction
to the New Testament, *The New Testament as Canon*
(1984), the product of five years' intensive research. It is
important to note that Childs readily concedes that the
historical-critical method has massive accomplishments to
its credit and remains an indispensable teacher. Yet it also
exhibits serious shortcomings as a tool for handling the
biblical text. In particular, it has failed to do justice to the
function of the New Testament as authoritative, canonical
literature of both an historical and a contemporary Christian community of faith and practice. For him the intentions
of authors or redactors, while not unimportant, are not of
primary importance. The meaning of a text inheres in the
text itself and in the setting within which it is read rather
than in the intentions of those who wrote it. As well as
asking what the text meant, we should ask what it means,
given that it is part of the canon of scripture.[12]

Irrelevant?

The criticisms of historical-critical exegesis which we have reviewed so far have been voiced by theologians, biblical scholars or scholars in other fields. But dissatisfaction with historical critical exegesis has been heard increasingly from another quarter, viz. from disgruntled preachers and students, who had hoped it would enable them to find a relevant message for proclamation, as well as clear guidance for social action, but whose hopes have not been realized. The commonest charge appears to be that even when the method does produce results which seem reasonably conclusive, those results all too often prove of little use for the practice of ministry or the living of the Christian life.

Ulrich Luz, in his inaugural lecture in Bern, identified this as the basic challenge facing interpreters of the Bible today, viz. the experience of countless pastors and students that their intensive engagement with the original meaning of a text made difficult, or even impossible, an answer to the question about the meaning of the text for the present. Instead of gaining, through the historical-critical method, a relevant message for contemporary proclamation, they have found themselves in a state of helplessness, stuck in the past, from which there no longer seems to be any viable way into the present. Hence the widespread impression that histor-ical-critical exegesis contributes nothing to the praxis of the church, the pastoral office or society. As examples of this split between historical-critical exegesis and contemporary praxis Luz cites first of all the extraordinary fascination exercised upon many theological students in Europe by Ernesto Cardenal's account of lay communities in Nicaragua which met with him to read the Bible and find in it a meaning for their lives, untroubled by the questions of the historical-critical method. Luz also cites the widening gap between scholarly exegesis and the homiletical interpreta-tion of the Bible. Until the Enlightenment, the scholarly and the homiletical interpretation of the Bible were closely related – witness, for example, the influence of the homilies of Chrysostom or the relationship between the lectures and sermons of Luther – but since the Enlightenment they have been diverging more and more, leading to a far-reaching divorce between text and sermon, as becomes apparent very often in homiletical practice and sometimes even in homiletical theory.[13]

To cite a witness to the same malaise from another continent, in *Transforming Bible Study* Walter Wink gives a vivid description of his growing awareness of a profound split between the academic study of the scriptures and the issues of life, first as a parish minister in south-east Texas and then as a teacher at Union Theological Seminary, New York. 'As a parish minister, I discovered', he writes, 'how isolated scholars had become from the pressures of living, how little of what they found fit to say had any applicability to preaching, to counselling, to the human struggles of those who regarded the Bible as somehow the key to life.'[14] When he returned to Union Seminary as a teacher, his sense of this malaise grew deeper.

In the face of challenges of such force as this, it would clearly be irresponsible simply to take the historical-critical method for granted. But what is to be said in reply? For the present we shall concentrate on the challenges posed by secular literary criticism and canonical criticism. The challenge identified by Luz and Wink will be taken up in Chapter 7.

The Intentional Fallacy

We begin with some comments on the genesis of the notion of 'The Intentional Fallacy'. That was the title of a highly influential New Critical essay published by W. K. Wimsatt and Monroe C. Beardsley in 1946,[15] a follow-up to an article which the same authors had contributed to a dictionary of world literature in 1945.[16] Critics who do not take the trouble to read these essays often assume that they were simply attacking the notion that the author's meaning represents the normative meaning, but in an essay published in 1968 entitled 'Genesis: A Fallacy Revisited', Wimsatt argues that that is a misreading of their intention. They were not denying that the author's meaning represents the normative meaning. They were rather maintaining that the surest evidence for that meaning, that authorial intention, is supplied by the work itself rather than by any clues we may pick up from our study of the author's life or even from the author's own statements in a journal or a letter or a reported conversation. Nor was it legitimate to use such external evidence to construct a theory of the author's intention in a particular work and then use that construct as a standard for assessing the value of what he had written. I quote a typical passage.

> What we meant in 1946 and what in effect I think we managed to say, was that the closest one could ever get to the artist's intending or meaning mind, outside his work, would be still short of his effective intention or operative mind as it appears in the work itself and can be read from the work. The intention outside the poem is always subject to the corroboration of the poem itself. No better evidence, in the nature of things, can be adduced than the poem itself.[17]

Their concern, in other words, was not to outlaw the author's meaning as the normative meaning but rather to rule out certain ways of establishing that meaning, and consequently certain ways of evaluating the author's work, as illegitimate.

An illustration should clarify the main point. Let us suppose that archaeologists unearthed in Ephesus a diary compiled by St Paul in which he referred to a letter he had just written to the Galatians and stated why he had written it. Even such a statement would still have to be tested and corroborated by the evidence of the letter itself.

But if this was their main point, then we have every right to do a Wimsatt-and-Beardsley, so to speak, on Wimsatt himself and not accept his own restatement as conclusive but subject it too to the test of corroboration by their original words. Whatever he may have thought they meant, the original essays provide the surest evidence for what they really meant. Do the original essays, therefore, bear out Wimsatt's restatement of their intention? The essay of 1946 appears to do so but not the article of 1945 in its entirety. The authors begin that article by distinguishing two meanings of 'meaning', the actual and the intentional. The former is defined as 'the meaning of the work itself', the latter as 'the meaning that the author intended to express in the work'. The actual meaning is then further defined as 'all that the ideal reader can find in it'. Later in the article they come close to identifying the actual meaning of a work with its intentional meaning but stop short of doing so, on the grounds that an author may use a word idiosyncratically, that is, with the intention of having it mean something which it cannot possibly mean. Yet towards the end they do appear to make this identification, so long as intentional meaning is redefined as 'the intent of the work'.[18]

However, even if Wimsatt and Beardsley did not set out to make a root-and-branch attack on authorial intention as a criterion of meaning, other people have done so. One thinks, for example, of Northrop Frye and of Roland Barthes and the whole Structuralist Movement. The question remains, therefore, 'What is the relationship between the meaning of a passage and the meaning intended by the original author?'

We have already noted an ambivalence in Wimsatt and Beardsley's article of 1945 in that one moment they appear to want to identify actual meaning with intentional meaning, the next to want to distinguish them. In this, I suggest, they speak for most of us. We are unwilling to dismiss the author's intentions as irrelevant to the meaning of what he has written and yet uneasy about limiting the full meaning of what he has written to the meaning which he explicitly intended.[19] Let us begin, then, by asking what is the nature of the nexus that we seem constrained to acknowledge between authorial meaning and actual meaning?

Not Logical but Ethical

The American scholar, E. D. Hirsch Jr, lays his finger on what I consider to be the nub of the matter when he argues in one of his many essays on this question that the nature of the nexus is not logical but ethical. The medieval interpreters who found Christian meanings in Homer and Virgil were standing on just as firm ground logically as Schleiermacher when he maintained that no text can legitimately mean at a later time what it could not have meant originally. If the *Aeneid* has been interpreted as a Christian allegory, that is unanswerable proof that such an interpretation is possible. Schleiermacher's norm of legitimacy is not deduced by logic but chosen. His preference for authorial meaning rests ultimately on an ethical choice. How does ethics come into it? Because we are aware of an obligation not to use the words of another person for our own purposes any more than we would use the person himself merely for our own ends.[20]

On these grounds Hirsch formulates the following maxim for interpretation, a maxim which he is careful to describe as ethical not logical: 'unless there is a powerful overriding value in disregarding an author's intention (i.e. original meaning), we who interpret as a vocation should not disregard it'.[21] This statement should not be seen as an affirmation of authorial intention as one criterion of meaning among others but as an affirmation of authorial privilege. In the same context he affirms 'a strong ethical presumption against anachronistic meaning'. In matters of meaning the author himself should be given the first word.

One argument which can be cited in support of Hirsch's thesis is the fact that the more anonymous a literary work is, the less we feel any constraint about altering its wording. It is the traditional folk-tale, which is anonymous by definition, which is transmitted in a variety of versions, precisely because (I suggest) no one, in retelling it, feels any obligation to an identifiable author.

I also draw support for Hirsch's position from Anthony Thiselton's recent advocacy of interpretative responsibility as a major and constructive hermeneutical category. Language, he argues, is a tool, and so we must always ask whether the use we are making of it is a responsible one. It is possible to make a text 'mean' whatever one wants it to mean, just as it is possible to use a chisel as a screwdriver or to use a piano for firewood. In each instance, however, the question must be asked, 'Is such an action responsible?'[22] Responsibility, let it be noted, is an ethical category.

Personal Texts

If Hirsch's argument is sound, it will follow that the obligation to respect authorial intention becomes the more binding the more personal the text, the more, that is, the text is stamped by the personality of the author, the more it is expressive of his beliefs and concerns. But, if so, then the obligation to respect authorial intention in interpreting the New Testament writings becomes inescapable, inasmuch as these writings are highly personal texts. Let us recall briefly the range of genres which they represent. Of the twenty-seven documents which make up the New Testament canon twenty-one have the form of a letter. There are also four Gospels. Then there is Acts and Revelation, which is probably best understood as an example of prophecy (see 1.3; 22.7,10,18f.). Common to all these writings, however, whatever their genre, is a conspicuously pastoral motivation. The writers whose work we have before us here are writing out of a concern for the spiritual welfare of definite communities of believers and a desire to speak to their needs.

Philemon   It is in the acknowledged letters of Paul that this personal motivation can be most clearly seen. Consider, for example, the shortest of them all, his letter to Philemon. Here is a letter from this person, Paul, to this person, Philemon, on behalf of a third person, Philemon's slave, Onesimus. Onesimus has run away from his master, apparently taking with him something of value (vv.18f.). Paul, who has somehow come across Onesimus and converted him to the faith, is now sending him back to his master with the request that Philemon should not only receive him as a brother but also send him back to Paul, as he has proved to be very useful to him (vv.13f.).

This document can fairly be described as an occasional writing, insofar as the occasion, as well as the author and the recipient, are clearly delineated for us. My summary may suggest that Paul's intention in writing the letter is equally clear. In fact, it can be debated whether Paul is actually requesting Philemon to send Onesimus back to him, and some have even argued that Paul is indirectly hinting to

Philemon that he should set Onesimus free. Be that as it may, there can be no question that this is a highly personal text.

The Other Letters of Paul What is true of Philemon is also largely true, with certain qualifications, of the Pauline Corpus as a whole. Each one of Paul's epistles, as they are usually called, is a genuine letter, written from this man, Paul, to this particular community, Galatia or Philippi or whatever. Each one can be rightly described as an occasional writing in the sense of having been occasioned by some development in the relationship between Paul and the community in question. Sometimes the letter is occasioned by a crisis that has arisen – the Galatians are succumbing to the propaganda of Judaizers, the Corinthians are, in the period covered by Paul's second epistle, in danger of being swayed by pseudo-apostles, who are trying to undo his work. Paul answers their attacks, point by point, and at times, as for example in Gal. 2.17 or I Cor. 10.23, even appears to turn their slogans against them. At other times Paul writes in response to a letter from the church concerned, as well as in response to verbal reports (I Corinthians) or to acknowledge a gift from the church (Philippians) or in order, among other things, to solicit the support of a church for a project he has in mind (Romans). What is true of all the letters is that they are pastorally motivated and therefore intensely personal texts. Indeed, with the possible exception of Cicero, Paul is probably better known to us through his writings than any other author of the ancient world.

The Epistles Alongside Paul's letters we have other writings which, though epistolary in form, do not appear to be genuine letters but tracts for the times intended for a wider circle of readers than a particular congregation. Indeed, there would seem to be a real point in reviving the distinction proposed by Deissmann between letters and epistles, and using the word 'letter' to describe those writings, like those of Paul's, which are genuine letters, while reserving the term 'epistle' for those writings in which the address is simply a literary device.[23] Yet these writings too are equally the expression of pastoral concern. Take Hebrews, for example.

Hebrews lacks an epistolary introduction, though it does have, in its present form at least, an epistolary ending. Quite a good case can be made for considering it as a treatise or sermon (cf. 13.22). What is clear, however, is that it is designed for a particular circle of readers in a particular spiritual condition. These readers have been Christians for many years, but their faith is in danger. The danger is not one of heresy or hypocrisy but of faith fatigue. This is showing itself in two ways. One is through their inadequate grasp of Christian truth. Since they are by no means recent converts, they ought by now to be capable of teaching others, but they are not. They have got stuck at an elementary level of understanding. They are in need of being taught all over again the ABC of God's revelation, in need of milk, when they should be having solid food (5.11f.). 'Dull of hearing' the author calls them in 5.11, with the implication that they have become dull of apprehension. The word which is translated 'dull' here and which is used again in 6.12 means feeble, slack, lazy, sluggish and denotes a condition which is the opposite of that of the trained athlete.

But signs of faith-fatigue are also apparent in their behaviour. They are in danger of losing heart. At some time in the past they had endured suffering for their faith (10.32–34). Some had been exposed to public abuse and affliction, and the rest had stood by them loyally, visiting them in prison, in spite of the risks which such action entailed. It had been a great contest, but they had undergone these sufferings as good athletes of Christ and had stood firm (10.32–34; cf. 6.9–10). Yet the author now has to exhort them continually to keep it up. Let them go on as they have begun. Let them not grow sluggish in action as they have already become in theological understanding (6.12). Let them maintain their zeal for the fulfilment of their hope right to the end (6.11). The last phrase is very emphatic, indicating where their weak point lay. Three times over the author urges them to hold fast to their confidence, their hope, their confession (3.6,14; 10.23; cf. 10.35). Staying power, 'stickability', is the quality of which they stand in the greatest need (10.36).

Therefore let them not grow weary or lose heart, like runners who collapse before the finishing post (12.3). Let them strengthen their drooping hands and paralysed knees (12.13). Let them not lose their glow.

The Testaments Compared   No doubt it could equally be said of most books of the Old Testament that in their final form, at least, they too have been shaped by pastoral concerns, but there are significant differences in the range of literary forms found within the two testaments. On the one hand, the Old Testament, in contrast to the New, contains a number of passages formally akin to myths, legends and folk tales. Barton observes that in dealing with such genres a structuralist approach, with its indifference to authorial intention, is an obvious strength, 'for whatever "meaning" a traditional folk-tale has can hardly be attributed to an "author" in any case: it must in some sense inhere in the tale itself'.[24] But a genuine letter like the letter to Philemon or a treatise like the epistle to the Hebrews represents something very different from a folk-tale. The one is a peculiarly personal means of communication, while the other is equally an expression of pastoral concern.

The Gospels and Acts   But what about the Gospels? And what about Acts? If we accept redaction criticism as an appropriate tool for the study of the Gospels – and who does not? – we are implicitly acknowledging that these writings too are highly personal texts, for it is the central contention of redaction criticism that the evangelists are to be regarded not merely as collectors of short bits and pieces of tradition but as authors in their own right with pronounced literary skills, theological perspectives and pastoral concerns. What is held to be true of the Gospels is also held of Acts, which, though unique in respect of its genre, is clearly the second volume of a two-volume work, of which the first volume is the Gospel of Luke.[25]

In attributing this insight primarily to redaction criticism, however, we need to recognize that there was redaction criticism before there were so-called redaction critics. Their work was in significant respects anticipated by several

writers, particularly W. Wrede and R. H. Lightfoot. The
significance of Lightfoot's contribution has been well
brought out by his pupil, Austin Farrer, who acknowledges
himself indebted to Lightfoot for the insight that 'the Gospel
of Mark is a genuine and profoundly consistent, complex act
of thought'. This discovery, he adds, comes like water in the
desert to those who have been trained to see in Mark's
Gospel 'a row of impersonal anecdotes strung together by a
colourless compiler'.[26]

Revelation What, finally of the book of Revelation? The
precise designation of the literary form of this book is itself
no easy task. On the one hand, it exhibits some epistolary
affinities. Not only does it contain seven letters in chapters 2
and 3, it begins with an epistolary prescript in 1.4 and ends at
22.21 with a wish which has the ring of an epistolary
conclusion. More important, though, is the fact that both at
the beginning and the end John describes his book as
prophecy (1.3; 22.7,10,18f.). As for the word 'apocalypse',
with which the first verse begins, this seems to be meant as
an indication of the book's contents rather than as a literary
classification.[27] But, however it be classified, this work too is
unmistakably motivated by pastoral concern. John the seer,
the prophet, is telling certain communities what he deeply
believes they urgently need to hear.

We have been discussing at some length the nature of the
nexus which most readers seem constrained to acknowledge
between authorial meaning and actual meaning and have
argued, following Hirsch, that the nature of this nexus is not
logical but ethical, so that it becomes the more binding, the
more personal the text. In accepting this argument, I am not
suggesting that the obligation to respect authorial meaning
is imposed only by personal texts. An impersonal document
from a legal authority would carry the same sort of obligation, but that would be because of the relationship between
the reader and the authority in question. My point is simply
that personal texts do entail such an obligation. I have also
argued that the New Testament texts must be seen as highly
personal texts, so that for the interpreter of the New
Testament the obligation to respect authorial intention

becomes inescapable. However, to acknowledge an obligation is one thing, to be able to fulfil it is another. In what I
have said so far I have implied, by my allusions to the
intentions of certain authors, that it is possible to ascertain,
with reasonable confidence, what aims they were pursuing in
writing as they did. Is that a presumptous assumption? How
realistic is it to try to determine the intentions of the New
Testament authors? This is an important question, which
calls for a full discussion.

Difference of Genre

It can be said at the outset that the task is a more or less
complex one, depending upon which genre one is dealing
with and which book one is reading.

By and large, it is not difficult to decide for whom Paul's
letters were intended or what aims he was pursuing in
writing them. This is not to say there is no room for debate.
For example, while it is clearly part of Paul's purpose in
Romans to pave the way for a visit to Rome, it is not entirely
clear to what extent the letter represents a response to the
actual situation of the Roman church. When Paul takes up
the problem of tension between the strong and the weak in
chapters 14 and 15, is he addressing an actual situation of
tension in the Roman church, of which he has heard reports,
or is he not?[28] However, there is still a great deal that can be
said about Paul's purpose in Romans and said with confidence.

But when we turn to the Gospels and Acts, the task
becomes more complex. We cannot 'read off' the intentions
of the evangelists from the Gospels as easily as we can read
off Paul's intentions in writing to Philemon from his letter of
the same name. Any judgments we may reach about the
intentions of the evangelists have to be more inferential. It is
true that the Gospels of Luke and John both contain a
definite statement of purpose, Luke at the beginning (1.1–4)
and John at the end (20.30f.), but these statements leave us
with important questions on our hands. Who, for example,
was the Theophilus referred to in Luke's preface and the
preface of Acts? And what exactly was his relationship to the

Christian church – new Christian or interested outsider?
The text of John 20.31, on the other hand, offers variant
readings, which have an important bearing on the interpretation of the author's stated purpose. Have these things been
written so that the readers may *come* to believe (reading the
aorist form of the verb, *pisteusēte*) or so that they may
continue to believe (reading the present tense, *pisteuēte*)?

It should also be recognized that there is more consensus
among scholars over the themes the evangelists are emphasizing than over the precise readership they have in mind
in making those emphases. For example, there can hardly be
any doubt that one of the themes Luke particularly wants to
emphasize in Acts is the God-given origin of the Gentile
mission. Episode after episode, from the story of Pentecost
on, seems designed to bring home to the reader that this was
the work of God. But to what sort of reader exactly? Is Luke
seeking to convince Roman officials, in the hope that they
will extend to the church the same toleration that was given
to the synagogue? Or is he addressing Christians who are
looking wistfully over their shoulders and ruefully wondering whether the Gentile mission, which had led to the final
separation between church and synagogue, had all been a
great mistake? Or again, is he trying to rehabilitate the
memory of Paul in the eyes of Christians who had been led to
believe that the great missionary to the Gentiles had been
deluded and that the whole Pauline heritage, of teaching as
well as practice, should be repudiated? One can find scholars
who are prepared to argue for each one of these positions.[29]

Nevertheless, we are not forced to resort to guesswork,
particularly in dealing with Matthew and Luke, because we
have access to some of the materials they had at their
disposal, and from our observation of the ways in which they
have used these materials we are able to draw certain
deductions about the overall purposes they were pursuing.
With Mark, if we assume, as most scholars do, that his was
the earliest Gospel, we do not enjoy that advantage. That is,
no doubt, one reason why so many theories about the
purpose of Mark have been canvassed in recent years. If we
knew more about the materials Mark had at his disposal, we
would be better able to judge what he was trying to do with

those materials. John Barton has pointed out that Old
Testament scholars face precisely the same problems trying
to assess the purposes of the various redactors, J, E, D and P,
who are widely held to be responsible for the final form of the
books of the Pentateuch. We do not have direct access to the
raw materials which these redactors had at their disposal. If
we did, we could say what their contribution had been, just
as we can say, broadly speaking, what the Chronicler has
done with his raw materials because we have most of his
sources in Samuel and Kings. The peculiar difficulty of the
Pentateuch is that we have only the finished product. Barton
then draws the following conclusion.

> In principle, then, Redaction Criticism is a perfectly
> reasonable approach; and in practice there are texts even in
> the Old Testament where it can be remarkably illumin-
> ating (I have instanced Chronicles). But more often
> than not, it is either unnecessary . . . or unsuccessful . . .
> The redactor's mind is far more opaque to us than we
> should like to think.[30]

Barton's main concern in this passage is to demonstrate
the limits of redaction criticism as a critical tool for the study
of the Old Testament. But in dealing with Matthew and Luke
we are dealing with writings more like Chronicles than the
Pentateuch, insofar as we do have access to an important
source used by Matthew and Luke, viz. Mark, and can also
draw some deductions from their use of the material common to them both but not derived from Mark, the material
usually designated by the symbol Q. I say 'some deductions'
because we must also allow for the possibility that Matthew
and Luke were using forms of the Q material which had
already diverged before their time.

Even with Mark, however, redaction criticism, though
more difficult, is by no means impossible. We can take note
of the material which he has chosen to include. There is no
reason to suppose that he, any more than John, has included
everything he knew, quite the opposite (cf. John 20.30;
21.25). Therefore if he has chosen to give prominence to
certain traditions, this suggests that he considered them
important and relevant, and any theory about the purposes of

his Gospel which fails to account for the prominence of these traditions can be pronounced inadequate.[31]

In the same way, theories about the sort of readers Luke had in mind in emphasizing the God-given origin of the Gentile mission in Acts can be evaluated according to their usefulness in accounting for the material Luke has actually included. If, as some have supposed, he is addressing Roman officials, the work has to be seen as primarily apologetic in intention, and then there is force in C. K. Barrett's comment that 'no official would ever have filtered out so much of what to him would be theological and ecclesiastical rubbish in order to reach so tiny a grain of relevant apology'.[32] As for the view that Luke is trying to counter polemic against Paul and rehabilitate his memory, that too labours under the difficulty of providing a plausible account of, at most, only a part of the material he has included. We can account more satisfactorily for the work as a whole if we suppose that he is addressing Christians who are looking wistfully over their shoulders and wondering ruefully whether the Gentile mission, which has led to the final separation between church and synagogue, has not been a great mistake.

Revelation

When we turn to the book of Revelation, we are confronted with problems of unusual difficulty. In relating his visions, John presents the reader with a whole succession of images – a beast with seven heads and ten horns, a lion that turns out to be a lamb, a river of blood 1600 stadia in length. Nor does the book consist merely of a series of static pictures. Things happen in the heavenly world to which John is transported. There is dialogue between John and his angelic guide. A scroll is opened. Horsemen ride forth. Trumpets are blown. Bowls are poured out. There is silence in heaven for about one hour (8.1).

The question with which the interpreter is constantly confronted is, 'What is one to make of this (presumably) symbolic language?' Many of these images have been interpreted in a whole variety of ways, all of which possess a certain plausibility. How can one be sure what the author 'meant'? Consider, for example, the silence in heaven, referred to in 8.1. Is this to be taken as a dramatic pause, intended to make even more impressive the judgments about to fall upon the earth?[33] Or as a return to the total silence which existed at creation?[34] Or as a pause in the singing of the heavenly choir to allow the prayers and praises of all God's people to be heard?[35] To be sure, even here a critical evaluation of these different theories can still be attempted in the light of John's distinctive emphases and the structure of the book as a whole. If the second explanation were right, for example, one would expect the incident to occur later, say, in chapter 20. But it is difficult, if not impossible, to reach a firm decision.

The State of the Question

Certainly it is true of Revelation, as also of all the other books in the New Testament, that new hypotheses are continually being put forward, yet I would maintain that the life-settings of most of the New Testament writings are already clear in outline. With the aid of the historical-critical method we can usually be confident of discerning, at least in broad detail, what the situation of those for whom the work was originally intended was like, how the author addressed their situation and how he would have been heard by them.[36] This is not to say, however, that there are no areas of study about which we would dearly like to know more. One of the ways in which the rapidly growing discipline of socio-economic historical analysis can illumine our study of the New Testament is by throwing more light on the actual social and economic situation of the addressees.[37]

Effective Intention

It also needs to be emphasized that in upholding the propriety of investigating authorial intention we are proposing as the primary goal of our investigation the meaning which the author intended to convey through the words he has chosen, not everything that was in his mind at the moment of composition. Whenever I write, I am usually attending to (I 'have in mind') meanings that are outside my subject of discourse, but these meanings are not available to anyone whose only access to my intentions is through my written words. Wimsatt, in the essay of 1968 referred to earlier, speaks of the artist's 'effective intention or operative mind as it appears from the work itself and can be read from the work'.[38] That more precise definition of authorial intention makes for greater clarity in the discussion.

Intention and Motive

We may also draw a useful distinction between authorial intention and authorial motive. In speaking of 'authorial intention', I have in mind the meaning (or, perhaps, better: the perception) which the author was seeking to communicate to his readers in and through the words he wrote; by 'authori..l motive' I mean the more ultimate purpose which he hoped to achieve by writing as he did. Thus, in telling the story of the wedding at Cana, John (I would propose) was seeking to present Christ to his readers as the one in whom the hopes of Israel found their fulfilment. His motive in so writing may well have been to persuade Jewish Christians who still retained links with synagogues to make up their minds, cross the road and throw in their lot once and for all with the church. However, while these two things may be distinguished in theory, they are in practice inseparable. In stressing the pastoral motivation of the New Testament writings, I have had authorial motive very much in mind.

The Acid Test – the Text

The question of how the task of probing the author's intention is best carried out will be considered from different angles in the next three chapters, but one point calls for special emphasis from the outset: any provisional understanding we may have of what an author is trying to communicate through a particular passage must be continually tested by what he has actually said and left unsaid. There is always a danger that we will notice those features of a passage which confirm our preconceptions of the author and ignore the rest. Inevitably and rightly (as we shall try to show more fully in Chapter 4, 'The Whole and Parts') we bring to any passage some conception of the author's purpose, but we must still read the text with eyes as wide open as we can force them, always ready for surprises. We must expose ourselves to the passage in all its particularity and allow it to make its maximum impact, always on the alert for anything which challenges or modifies or even contradicts our preconceptions. The acid test of any interpretation, whether ours or anyone else's, is, 'Does it do justice to the passage as text?'

Every biblical interpreter would do well to heed the following definition by F. R. Leavis of the aim of the literary critic:

> The critic's aim is, first, to realise as sensitively and completely as possible this or that which claims his attention. . . . He must be on his guard against abstracting improperly from what is in front of him and against any premature or irrelevant generalising – of it or from it. His first concern is to enter into possession of the given poem (let us say) in its concrete fulness.[39]

The need for the biblical interpreter to take such words to heart should become clearer in the next section.

The main question with which we are presently concerned is how realistic it is to attempt to ascertain the intentions of the New Testament authors. By way of a preliminary general comment, I have been trying to show that the task is a more or less complex one, depending upon which genre one is dealing with and which book one is reading. There are, however, other difficulties which, while they confront any reader of an ancient text, ought to be of particular concern to the reader of the Bible.

Effective-History

There is first of all the fact that we bring to the text which we are seeking to interpret a whole set of presuppositions, with the result that the text does not meet us, so to speak, as a naked text but as a text already clothed with associations. This comes about not only because it has been subjected to

continual interpretation, in commentaries and other theological writings, during the intervening centuries but because it has also worked its way into history in other ways;
for example, in sermons and liturgies, in hymnody and art, in
personal decisions and church law, in wars and in works of
merciful love.[40] This long tradition of effective-history
inevitably influences our reading of the text. As Ulrich Luz
puts it, the exegete is not like a chemist, examining the
composition of water in a laboratory, but more like a sailor,
who is himself borne up and carried along by the very water
of the river which he is seeking to investigate.[41]

Here are two simple examples of how our reading of a text
is influenced by its effective-history. Centuries of associating the name 'Samaritan' with the epithet 'good' make
it extraordinarily difficult for us to feel the impact of the
word 'Samaritan' on Jesus's first hearers. Centuries of
associating the word 'Pharisee' with legalism and even
hypocrisy make it equally difficult for us to feel the impact of
that word on his first hearers.

Change of Setting

A further difficulty in the way of the interpreter seeking to
ascertain the intention of the original author is the fact that
he or she lives in a different life-setting. This is not to say that
the situation of the first readers of a New Testament writing
may not be comparable in important respects with ours – in
our last chapter we shall be seeking to show that this often
proves to be true – what is being maintained is that our
situation can never be precisely the same as theirs. Moreover, we live in a culture which is, in significant respects,
different from theirs.[42] These differences may make it
extremely difficult for us to recapture the full impact of a
passage we are reading upon its first readers. For example, it
is extremely difficult for those of us who are not observant
Jews to feel the full impact of Paul's declaration that Christ is
the end of the law (Rom. 10.4) upon people for whom the
abiding validity of the law was a self-evident truth and to
whom the deliberate breaking of the law appears to have
presented itself not so much as something wrong as some-

thing simply impossible. Again, one reason why many modern readers have difficulty in understanding apocalyptic is that they have never lived under a totalitarian regime. The image of a power taking its seat in the temple of God and usurping his prerogative is strange to them.

Insuperable?

These difficulties which we have been discussing, difficulties due to the effective-history of the biblical writings and to our changed life-setting, can certainly be alleviated. To take up again the difficulties created for us by the effective-history of the passage we are reading, it is possible for us to take account of the influence exercised upon us by traditional interpretations as well as by all the other forms in which these texts have entered into our history and helped to make us the people we are. As Luz puts it, adapting a phrase of Lessing, we cannot leap over the 'nasty, wide ditch' separating us from the first century as though it did not exist, but we can climb down into the ditch and at least climb some distance up the other side again.[43]

We may not be able to rid our minds entirely of the associations clinging to words like 'Samaritan' or 'Pharisee' but we can go a long way towards doing so.

As for the fact that some writings of the New Testament are addressed to life-settings to which our experience affords no parallel, this difficulty can to some extent be overcome by reading the works of modern writers who have stood near to where those first readers stood and can therefore enable us to enter imaginatively into their situation. We may not know at first hand what it is like to be brought up as Jews living under the Law but through the writings of recent Jewish authors like Elie Wiesel or Isaac Bashevis Singer or Chaim Potok or Victor Gollancz we can begin to understand what it means. My own description in an earlier paragraph of the authority exercised by the Law over the mind and heart of the observant Jew owes a good deal to the autobiography of Victor Gollancz.[44] In the same way, writers from countries like Soviet Russia or East Germany can help us to begin to understand what it means to live under a totalitarian regime.

Besides, there is always the possibility that our own circumstances may change, thrusting us into a situation in which passages which had hitherto meant little to us suddenly become luminous with meaning. Many Christians who suffered persecution at the hands of the Nazis found passages in the Bible which had hitherto had little to say to them suddenly speaking with a new voice. In her description of Ravensbruck prison camp Corrie Ten Boom speaks for many.

> As the rest of the world grew stranger, one thing became increasingly clear, and that was the reason the two of us were here. . . . From morning until lights out, whenever we were not in ranks for roll call, our Bible was the centre of an ever-widening circle of help and hope. Like waifs clustered around a blazing fire, we gathered about it, holding out our hearts to its warmth and light. The blacker the night around us grew, the brighter and truer and more beautiful burned the word of God.
>
> Who shall separate us from the love of Christ? Shall tribulation or distress or persecution or famine or nakedness or peril or sword? . . . Nay, in all these things we are more than conquerors through him that loved us.
>
> I would look about us as Betsie read, watching the light leap from face to face. More than conquerors. . . . It was not a wish. It was a fact. We knew it, we experienced it minute by minute – poor, hated, hungry. We are more than conquerors. Not we shall be. We are!
>
> Sometimes I would slip the Bible from its little sack with hands that shook, so mysterious had it become to me. It was new; it had just been written. I marvelled sometimes that the ink was dry. I had believed the Bible always but reading it now had nothing to do with belief. It was simply a description of the way things were – of hell and heaven, of how man acts and how God acts.[45]

The difficulties created by the effective-history of the New Testament texts and our changed life-setting should not be exaggerated. Neither, on the other hand, should they be lightly set aside. We can surely acknowledge that there is some truth in Gadamer's contention that we understand a work in a different way from its original author if we understand it at all.[46]

The Wider Meanings of 'Meaning'

Moreover, we should be able to begin to see why the meaning intended by the original author, even if it can be ascertained with reasonable confidence, should not be seen as exhausting the meaning of the passage. Earlier in this chapter, in posing the question of the relationship between authorial meaning and actual meaning, I stated it as my conviction that while most of us feel constrained to acknowledge a certain obligation to authorial meaning we are also unwilling to limit the meaning of a text to the meaning explicitly intended by the author. We have discussed at some length the nature of this widely acknowledged obligation to authorial meaning and have also discussed at some length the difficulties confronting the interpreter seeking to recover it. Now we must turn our attention to further components of meaning which are barely, if at all, authorial.

Barely Conscious Meaning

We begin with what may be called barely conscious or unattended meaning. I used the expression 'explicitly intended' a moment ago, because there are usually components of an author's intended meaning which he is not conscious of. Indeed, if his meaning is complicated, he can hardly be paying attention to all its complexities at any given moment. What I have in mind here is the turn of phrase which is unlikely to be the result of careful deliberation yet is readily recognized by anyone well versed in the thought of the author concerned as revealing and characteristic. For example, Paul's fourfold use of 'us' and 'our' in Gal. 1.3f., is probably unconscious yet still indicative of his desire not to exclude the Galatians, for all their folly, from the community of faith and love.[47] The maxim of Hirsch's which we quoted earlier, that, unless there is a powerful overriding value in disregarding an author's intention, we who interpret as a vocation should not disregard it, does not necessitate the

Striking Home

exclusion of such unattended or barely conscious meanings from the meaning of the passage as a whole. They can be regarded as unconscious implicates of the author's intention.

Shining in a New Light

But Hirsch's maxim is worded in such a way as to allow us to include in the meaning of a passage even more than these barely conscious meanings. The need for a wide definition of the meaning of 'meaning' will become more apparent if we consider further the implications of reading a passage at a later time and in a new life-setting. I spoke earlier of the ways in which such differences of perspective can make it difficult for us to feel the full impact of a passage on its first hearers. But that is not the whole story. The changed perspective from which we read a text may impoverish our understanding of it. It may, on the other hand, enrich our understanding.

First of all, from our later vantage point we are able to read a text in the light of all of its author's extant writings and therefore sometimes are able to see how an apparently casual phrase encapsulates the essential thrust of his work as a whole. Elsewhere I have tried to show that the heart of Paul's theology is encapsulated in half of a verse, viz. II Cor. 1.9b: '. . . to make us rely not on ourselves but on God who raises the dead.'[48]

Furthermore, through being read in a new life-setting, a passage may shine in a new light and disclose depths of meaning of which the original author could not have been aware. This is not just a matter of us coming to see better what an original author was getting at. The text itself acquires a new level of meaning.

For example, John 1.18 speaks of Christ having made the invisible God known. Anyone reading the text in Greek could hardly fail to notice that the verb John uses for 'made known' is cognate with a word which we have taken over into English in transliterated form and which indeed forms the theme of the present book, the word 'exegesis'. Can we not speak of Christ therefore as the exegesis of God? Such a statement is surely fully consistent with John's intention in this passage. Yet it conveys to the modern reader all sorts of implications of which John himself can have had no inkling.[49]

Furthermore, apart from unconscious motivation and the new dimensions of meaning disclosed by a text when read in a new life-setting, there is also the fact of the rich variety of meaning implicit in all great literature. All great literature abounds in images, metaphors, symbols, but, as we shall see in the next chapter, no apt image, metaphor or symbol is reducible without remainder to a simple statement. Is it not a mark precisely of an inspired author, to use the word 'inspired' in the most general sense, that he or she is able to grasp intuitively the aptness of this image in this context without consciously apprehending the fullness of meaning which it is capable of conveying?[50] Plato, in a well-known passage, has Socrates relate how he found poets to be 'like prophets and oracular persons, who say many fine things without knowing what it is that they are saying'.[51] If this is true of writings commonly recognized as 'inspired' in the most general sense, then Christians have still more reason for holding it to be true of those writings which they believe to be in some sense inspired by the Holy Spirit.[52]

It can be argued that the biblical writers themselves give us clear warrant for believing that they themselves were wiser than they knew. Consider, for example, the way in which all the writers of the New Testament claim to find, all through the Old Testament, prophecies of the events of the gospel. Some of the passages which they claim to see fulfilled in this way prove, when examined in their original context, to be clearly predictive passages. One can cite, for example, the Servant Songs of Deutero-Isaiah. But, equally clearly, other passages are not. Hosea 11.1, for example, quoted by Matthew in Matt. 2.15 as a prediction of the sojourn of the holy family in Egypt, clearly refers in its original context to the Exodus. Are we to suppose that Matthew believed that Hosea, in uttering these words, was aware that they also bore a predictive meaning? Or did he believe that Hosea was, thanks to the inspiration of the Holy Spirit, wiser than he knew? The second explanation seems much more likely, especially in the light of a passage like I Cor. 6.9f., where Paul interprets the command that an ox is not to be muzzled when

treading out the grain as a reference to the maintenance of
the Christian ministry. If we do not take the view that Paul
believed Moses to have been wiser than he knew, we have to
suppose that Paul attributed to him the deliberate use of a
peculiar kind of code. But if the New Testament authors
believed that the writers of the Old Testament were wiser
than they knew, why should they not have held the same
belief about themselves, convinced, as they were, that the
Holy Spirit was active among them in a new and unpara-
llelled way?

Meaning or Significance?

Granted, then, that the biblical writings are always liable
suddenly to become contemporary by disclosing some fresh
application, how are we to describe such fresh applications,
as part of the meaning of the passage or not? In my judgment,
they can fairly be described as further levels of meaning,
distinct from the meaning intended by the original author
but nevertheless part of the meaning of the passage in
question. Some scholars prefer to use the word 'significance'
to refer to this power of all true classics to speak afresh to a
new situation,[53] but I consider that term less appropriate, in
view of its widespread use since Frege with reference to the
evaluation of a text as distinct from the determination of its
meaning.[54]

An Infinite Process?

But, it may be argued, once we extend the meaning of the
passage to include senses of which the original author could
not have been aware, where do we stop? Are there not likely
to be as many readings of a text as there are readers of it?

In order to avoid the either-or of a closed concept of
meaning on the one hand and a totally open concept on the
other, some critics extend the criterion of authorial intention by distinguishing between new meanings which are
genuinely implicit in a text and those which are arbitrarily
imported into it. For a new meaning to count as genuinely
implicit in a text, one must be able, without difficulty, to

conceive of the author accepting it, had he had the opportunity to consider it. For our interpretation of John to be controlled by John's intention, it is not necessary that it should have occurred to John in very much the same terms but rather that we should be able to envisage him assenting to it, once its terms had been made familiar to him.[55] The statement that Christ is the exegesis of God would be an example of such an interpretation.

Subconscious Motivation?

While the position which I have just outlined is an attractive one, it does not seem to do justice, however, to the phenomenon of subconscious motivation. By that I mean not the unattended meaning which the author would have gladly acknowledged, had it been brought to his attention, but the meaning which he, in all probability, would have repudiated, had he learned of it being attributed to him, but which nevertheless seems to be present in the text. Literary critics sometimes speak of an author subverting his own text. We may simply say that he seems to be arguing against himself. By that we mean that in the process of seeking to communicate something to his readers he also appears to be saying something else alongside of, and even incompatible with, his (expressed or presumed) conscious intention. The desire to say that 'something else' is subconscious; it has, in fact, been repressed from consciousness, because it is in conflict with his dominant intention.

The classic example in English literature of an author subverting his own text is Milton in *Paradise Lost*. It was Dryden who first observed that the real hero of the poem is the devil. As Blake put it, Milton was of the devil's party without knowing it. Had a contemporary of Milton's been able to put it to him that the devil was the real hero of the poem, it is hard to imagine Milton doing anything but repudiate the suggestion, and yet the poem itself bears its own evidence to the contrary. Whatever Milton is likely to have insisted that he meant, the poem witnesses to a further subconscious level of meaning.[56]

Graham Hough finds an analogy to the phenomenon of

subconscious motivation in literature in the involuntary, symptomatic gesture. 'He said, "Of course I don't care for her any more", but as he said it his voice broke.'[57] The breaking voice is not consciously intended but nevertheless revealing of the speaker's true feelings. Similar effects can occur in literature.

It may be that it is in this way that we can best account for some of the apparent contradictions in Paul's statements in I Corinthians on the status of women in the churches. It has often been observed that whereas in certain passages in I Corinthians, notably 7.3–4 and 11.11, Paul speaks of men and women being in every way equal in Christ, in line with his declaration in Gal. 3.28, in other passages, particularly I Cor. 11.3 and 7, he seems to entertain the concept of a hierarchical order in which woman is subordinate to man.

It is, of course, possible that the traditional interpretation of the two latter passages is mistaken. For example, when Paul describes woman in verse 7 as the 'glory of man', he may not be thinking of woman *reflecting* man's glory, as is often supposed, since, as Feuillet has shown, the evidence for *doxa* bearing the sense of 'reflection' is non-existent, but may rather be thinking of her, in accordance with Gen. 2.23, as the one who represents man's joy and pride by bringing him an incomparable wealth of which he would otherwise be deprived.[58]

On the other hand, it is difficult to eliminate all notion of subordination from verse 3, so that the best explanation of the apparent contradictions in this chapter may be that Paul is arguing against himself and that in the course of upholding the right of women to pray and prophesy publicly, so long as they do not let their hair down, he has recourse in verse 3 to the notion of a descending hierarchy – God, Christ, man, woman – a notion which is in fundamental conflict with the intention of the passage as a whole but which appeals to a latent desire in his own mind to keep women in their place. On this view, we are dealing in this passage with an interplay of authorial motivations of whose complexity, and indeed contrariety, Paul himself was not aware. If that is correct, it would follow, of necessity, that in order to do justice to such a passage it is not sufficient to confine our attention to the question, 'What was Paul seeking to convey to his readers through this passage?' We must also reckon with the possibility of subconscious motivation.

Catalysts of Communication

Nor is it sufficient to confine our attention to the author's intentions, whether conscious or subconscious. It is a source of continual astonishment to some writers and speakers, particularly preachers, to discover how often they are perceived as saying something other than what they thought they were saying. It is the writer or speaker who appears to be arguing against himself who, above all, lays himself open to such misapprehension. It is therefore appropriate, particularly when we are dealing with a document like a letter, which is addressed to a particular addressee, to consider it not only as the expression of its author's intentions, whether conscious or not, but also as the catalyst of a process of communication, which may have followed a course quite different from that envisaged by the author himself. It is considerations such as these which have led to the development of what is called in English Reception Theory or Reader-Response Theory. This may be defined as the systematic study of the act of communication from the standpoint of both author and recipients.[59]

If Paul is in fact arguing against himself in I Cor. 11.2–16, it would not be surprising if different groups among his hearers heard only the parts which they wanted to hear, his liberal readers hearing only his liberal sentiments, his conservative readers only his conservative sentiments. This may help to explain why a conservative estimate of the role of women is implicitly attributed to Paul in the Deutero-Pauline literature (see Eph. 5.22–24; Col. 3.18; I Tim. 2.12; Titus 2.5) and probably put into Paul's mouth in I Cor. 14.33b–36.[60]

Subconscious Motivation and Intentionality

Does Hirsch's maxim permit us to take into account the phenomenon of subconscious motivation? Yes, though it does not refer to it explicitly. If the subconscious meanings are reckoned to be part of the original meaning, then clearly they are not to be disregarded. If they are not counted as part of the original meaning, then Hirsch's escape clause would permit us to take them into account on the grounds that at this point we believe we understand the author better than he understood himself.

Canonical Meaning?

Hirsch's maxim was proposed as a ruling on the kind of weight to be given to authorial intention, not as an exhaustive description of the procedure to be followed in the exegesis of the New Testament. A procedure which took into account the various additional levels of meaning which we have identified so far in this chapter would necessarily comprise several steps and include some such rubrics as the following:

Besides seeking to ascertain the meaning which the original author was trying to communicate to the readers he had in view, you should be alert to barely conscious or unattended meanings and to subconscious meanings. You should also ask whether the passage shines in a new light through being read in a new life-setting.

I would also argue for the recognition of yet another level of meaning, one which arises out of interaction between the text and the framework or horizon within which it is in fact read, viz. the canon of scripture. In recognizing this level of meaning, I am concurring with the basic standpoint of Brevard Childs, not indeed to the point of finding the intentions of authors or redactors of only peripheral interest but to the extent of seeing the meaning of a text inhering not only in the text itself but also in the setting within which it is read.

It should also be noted that Childs is not arguing that the historical-critical method should be discarded but rather that it be complemented by a qualified acceptance of a basic assumption which was accepted without question by interpreters of the biblical text from the second century to the eighteenth, viz. that the individual biblical text was to be understood from the standpoint of the totality of the faith, whether that was seen as embodied in the *regula fidei*, gnostic illumination, the church's teaching or the reformed faith. It is this basic contention of Childs which I support.[61]

His position may well commend itself more strongly, if we reflect on the tenacity with which a particular interpretation of a particular parable has been held throughout most of Christian history, viz. the parable of the good Samaritan. Since Jülicher's great work on the parables, published in 1899, this parable has usually been understood as an illustrative story, which demonstrates what love means in action. It does not ask 'Who is my neighbour?' but goes out to anyone who crosses my path and needs my help. Patristic exegetes, however, from the earliest time to which the sources take us, viz. the second half of the second century, are united in interpreting this parable allegorically and christologically; that is, the good Samaritan represents him who came down to a wounded humanity with healing and deliverance, Christ himself. This interpretation seems to have been universal right up to the end of the medieval period and remained dominant, particularly in sermons and devotional literature, until the end of the nineteenth century.[62]

Sometimes the allegorization is carried to extraordinary lengths, as when the innkeeper is seen as standing for St Paul or St Peter, and the two coins for baptism and holy communion or the two Testaments or the double love command, yet there is surely an intrinsic rightness about seeing in the helpless, wounded traveller a picture of fallen humanity, in the priest and Levite a picture of false shepherds of Israel and in the Good Samaritan a picture of the Good Shepherd, Christ himself. Such an interpretation seems to have an intrinsic propriety when the parable is read in the light of the Bible as a whole.[63]

It is important to realize that a deeper theological justification can be offered for a christological reinterpretation of the parables than a mere similarity between the role of Christ and that of the Good Samaritan in the parable of the same name. As I shall try to show in the next chapter, the parables are not simply a linguistic tool which Jesus chose to use in order to talk about the kingdom, they are a means of its coming, a means by which it becomes a reality in our lives. But, according to Jesus's teaching, the kingdom has also drawn near to the world in his own actions (Matt. 11.11f.; 12.28,38–42 and pars). This means that his proclamation, largely through parables, of the nearness of the kingdom and his actions are closely related to each other. As Hans Weder puts it, 'While the actions of Jesus are a commentary on his parable proclamation, his proclamation is the explanation of his actions.'[64]

From this it follows that the parables are indissolubly bound up with the person of Jesus himself. They derive an essential part of their truth from him. It is in him that they find their embodiment, in him that they are true. Therefore when we find in some parables that Jesus himself has been taken up into the story in the course of transmission (see e.g. Matt. 22.1–14; Mark 12.1–12 and pars; cf. John 10.1–18) it is inappropriate to dismiss these developments as allegorical corruption. On the contrary, such a christological reinterpretation of the parables is entirely appropriate. He *is* the son of the king, the son of the landowner, the good shepherd.

In the latter part of this chapter we have found several reasons for defining the meaning of a passage in wider terms than those of authorial intention alone. There is the turn of phrase which is unlikely to be the result of careful deliberation but is nevertheless revealing. Because of the phenomenon of subconscious motivation, the author may have said, and may have been perceived as saying, more than he was conscious of saying. Through being read in the light of the author's total work, the text may acquire a new depth. Through being read in a new life-setting, it may shine in a new light, by lending itself to some fresh application. And, finally, the text may acquire a further level of meaning in the light of the total biblical witness. But if it is to yield this enhanced luminosity, these deeper resonances, the exegete must bring to it the appropriate questions. One cannot limit oneself to the question, 'What was this author trying to convey through this passage to the readers he had in view?'

Reassessment in the Light of the Gospel

One must also be prepared to ask a critical question of a different order, viz. 'When I read this passage in the light of the Bible as a whole or, more fundamentally, in the light of God's revelation in Christ, do I find that it calls for some sort of qualification?'

Let it be noted in passing that in framing the question in this precise way we are implying that the ultimate authority for Christian faith and life is not the Bible itself but the living word of God, to whom it bears witness and who speaks through it. Related to this question, which is too big to examine in detail here, is the question of the legitimacy of systematic theology. If the ultimate authority for Christian faith were simply the Bible, one could hardly justify the existence of systematic theology as a discipline distinct from biblical theology. In fact, however, as James D. G. Dunn points out, systematic or dogmatic theology, not least in the creeds and confessions it has produced, has always gone beyond biblical theology in content, as well as in structure and aim.[65]

To revert to the question itself, what we now have in mind is a different kind of perception from that which we have just been discussing. The kind of perception which we have just been discussing was essentially the perception of multiple layers of meaning: by reading this passage in the light of the Bible as a whole, we discern in it a new depth. The kind of perception we now have in mind is rather the perception of contrariety: by reading this passage in the light of the gospel we are constrained to say 'Yes, but . . . The things that this author appears to be saying here need to be qualified in the light of the total biblical message, as I perceive it. The truth to which he is seeking to bear witness is bigger than this.'

Sachkritik

This kind of critical reflection is sometimes described by the German word 'Sachkritik', that is, content criticism. Content criticism is concerned with the question how far this passage does justice to the heart of the matter (in German: *die Sache*), that is, to the kerygma, the gospel, as it is witnessed to not only by this same author but by the New Testament as a whole.[66] In the choice of this designation for this particular kind of critical reflection one can detect the

influence of Barth's plea, referred to earlier, for a commentary which grapples with 'the enigma of the matter' (*die
Sache*). *Sachkritik* may appear to be a presumptuous under-
taking, but there will be times when we are driven to it by
loyalty to the gospel as we perceive it.

As an illustration of *Sachkritik* I cite Eduard Schweizer's
discussion of the episode of the guard at the grave in his
commentary on Matthew (Matt. 27.62–66).[67] What is especially striking about Schweizer's discussion is the way in
which he both questions the road along which Matthew has
encouraged later writers to go by presenting the resurrection
in the way that he has in this passage *and* acknowledges that
the very story which Matthew is telling judges Matthew's
own use of it. Considered as an historical report, the story of
the bribing of the guard bristles with difficulties and is likely
to owe its origin to apologetic concerns. The statement in
28.15, along with other references by second-century Christian writers, shows that one of the ways in which the Jewish
leaders tried to discredit the resurrection message was by
asserting that the disciples had stolen the body. It would not
be surprising if, in the struggle to refute this story, a counter-
explanation was put forward, and gained credence, that there
had been a Jewish conspiracy to suppress the evidence.
Nevertheless, in repeating this explanation, Matthew comes
close to suggesting that the fact of the resurrection was
objectively demonstrated in such a way as to expose unbelief
as sheer unwillingness to believe. Insofar as he does, however, he runs counter to the rest of the New Testament.
Throughout the New Testament there is a consistent refusal
to present the appearances of the risen Christ as spectacular
miracles which could have been watched with amazement
by anyone. For example, in all three accounts of the appearance to Paul in Acts it is Paul alone who grasps the inner
meaning of the encounter. Matthew himself clearly implies
that even the appearance of Christ on the mountain was not
so overwhelming as to leave no room for doubt. 'And when
they saw him' we read in 28.17, 'they worshipped him; but
some doubted.' This is in marked contrast to the later,
apocryphal Gospel of Peter, in which Gentiles soldiers and
Jewish elders become eyewitnesses of the resurrection,

which now becomes an historical fact which can be established incontestably.

It is because he sees Matthew encouraging the development in this direction that Schweizer writes that 'this story marks the first step along a road that runs counter to the witness of the bible'.[68] But at the same time Schweizer also adds the following comment.

> Believers can experience the reality of the Risen One only by letting him take them with him along the road of discipleship. Indeed, they know something of what can still be discerned even in Matthew's wrong-headed narrative. Through these very verses there still resounds something of the laughter of God, which breaks through tombs which have been barricaded, sealed and guarded by soldiers, overcoming all the undertakings and manipulations of men.[69]

Including, we may add, Matthew's own attempt to present the resurrection as a provable event. Thus Matthew is himself contributing to that deeper insight into the resurrection by which his own use of this story can be judged. This is what is meant by *Sachkritik*.

A Never Ending Process?

Before we bring this chapter to a close, it is appropriate that we should take up once more a question which has already been raised but not yet fully answered, viz. Is the interpretation of the New Testament, and indeed of the Bible as a whole, a never-ending process? If we admit as constitutive of the meaning of a passage its capacity to shine in a new light when read at a later time and in a new life-setting, the answer has to be, yes. To quote one of the most influential recent writers on hermeneutics, H. G. Gadamer:

> The discovery of the true meaning of a text or a work of art is never finished, it is in fact an infinite process. Not only are fresh sources of error constantly excluded, so that the true meaning has filtered out of it all kinds of things that obscure it, but there emerge continually new sources of

understanding, which reveal unsuspected elements of meaning.[70]

To acknowledge this, however, is not to say that we are totally without guide-lines. While I have gone out of my way not to limit the meaning of a passage to the meaning intended by the original author, I still hold to the principle of authorial privilege. While unwilling to allow the author the last word, I still wish to give him the first word. But how are these two emphases to be held in balance?

Perspectival Meaning

Ulrich Luz may well be pointing us towards an answer with his concept of *'Richtungssinn'*, a word which might be translated 'perspectival meaning'. It is true, he argues, that biblical texts have a firm kernel of meaning. One can state, for example, what Paul was seeking to communicate by a particular statement and how it was understood by his first readers. Yet the meaning of the biblical texts, like that of many other texts, particularly poetical texts, can never be captured once for all in a definitive definition. For, along with a kernel of meaning, these texts also have a kind of perspectival meaning, which makes possible the continual disclosure of new meaning.

We have already noted Luz's concern here to avoid either a totally static or a totally fluid understanding of meaning. Something which is equally noteworthy is his emphasis on *praxis*. For Luz, *Richtungssinn* is an essentially dynamic concept. The biblical texts have the character of sign-posts. They both direct and empower the reader to walk along a way, to adopt new attitudes, a definite *praxis*. It is to those who walk along that new way that they disclose again and again new meaning. The biblical message is meant to be grasped by new people in what is again and again a new situation and each time to be interpreted anew through their life.[71]

Retrospect and Prospect

In the course of this chapter we have touched on several topics which call for fuller treatment. One is the importance of literary form. That will be the theme of the next chapter.

Another is the delicate balance and interaction between one's understanding of a book as a whole and one's understanding of individual paragraphs, between one's understanding of a passage as a whole and one's understanding of its component parts. That will be the subject of the following chapter.

A third problem which is beginning to emerge has to do with the dimension of time. What is the relationship between the meaning which is being conveyed by this word in this passage and the meanings which it conveyed in earlier texts? Or between the understanding of a theological concept that comes to expression in this passage and earlier understandings of that concept? These questions will be the subject of a further chapter.

Another issue which has been raised in this chapter but not yet dealt with arises from the complaint of many pastors and students that even when we can ascertain to our own satisfaction the 'meaning' of a biblical passage, as intended by the original author or however it may be defined, it often proves to be of little use for the practice of ministry. This is an issue which I will take up in the last chapters of the book, where we turn our attention to preaching.

3

The Typical and the Unique: The Importance of Genre

The question with which we were mainly concerned in the previous chapter was, what weight should be given in matters of exegesis to authorial intention? Our conclusion, in brief, was that while the author should not be allowed the last word, he should certainly be given the first word. At more than one point we touched on the question of literary form or genre.

From the outset I was concerned to emphasize that an exegesis of a passage will always differ from a paraphrase of it, but I observed in passing that the degree of difference will vary, depending on the type of passage one is dealing with, in other words, the genre. An exegesis of a passage of argument may not differ very much from a paraphrase; with narrative or parable the difference between paraphrase and exegesis is likely to be more marked.

Later in the chapter I raised the question, is it possible to ascertain, with reasonable confidence, the aims which the various New Testament authors were pursuing? The first part of my answer was that the task is a more or less complex one, depending upon which genre one is dealing with and which book one is reading. We shall now examine the importance of genre in greater detail.

The word itself is derived ultimately from the Latin word 'genus', which, besides meaning birth, race or offspring, is widely used in all periods and kinds of Latin literature to mean kind, sort, class or order. As used in modern English (or French, from which it is directly taken), it denotes a literary or artistic type or style. The word is a comparative newcomer to the vocabulary of English literary criticism, having established itself only at the beginning of this century. Earlier authors spoke of literary kinds or species.

The main thesis of the present chapter can be stated quite simply: as the form in which the writer expresses himself varies, so should the manner in which one handles what he has written. But this is not all. In speaking of genres at all, we are implying that some writings have so much in common that they can be considered as different examples of the one form of literary expression. Nor are such similarities fortuitous. They are due to the authors concerned having followed certain recognized literary conventions. The way in which we write is always influenced to some extent by the ways in which other writers before us have expressed themselves in writing, just as our decision to use this word to express our meaning is always influenced by the way in which it is used by the community of speakers of which we are part. If the way in which we expressed ourselves were totally unrelated to existing conventions of self-expression, our hearers or readers would be at a loss to know what to make of what we were saying, just as much as they would be if we chose to use a word in a way quite unrelated to current usage. Thus genre has been described by Frank Kermode as 'a context of expectation, the equivalent, for a longer discourse, of the set of expectations which enables us to follow a sentence as it is spoken'; and again as 'a consensus, a set of fore-understandings exterior to a text which enables us to follow that text, whether it is a sentence, a book or a life'.[1] At the same time a good deal of confusion has been caused in biblical studies by over-zealous classification, by ruthless tidying, by forcing different writings into rigidly defined categories. There is always a certain artificiality about classifying a writing according to its genre, in so far as by doing so we necessarily leave out of account whatever is unique about the writing in question. For example, every one of the commonly acknowledged letters of Paul can be assigned to the genre, letter, yet precisely because each one is a letter, a genuine letter addressed to a particular circle of readers in a particular situation, each has its own distinctive character. Moreover, within each letter one finds a considerable variety of style.

Furthermore, one must always be open to the possibility that a writer may be deliberately deviating from a conventional literary form or even creating a new form.

In a word, therefore, what the critical reader needs always to aim at is a feel for this writing not only in its similarity to other writings but also in its uniqueness. These are questions which I shall take up in the latter part of the chapter.

One further point needs clarification before we proceed. In speaking of genre and the ways in which writers are influenced by literary conventions, 'contexts of expectations' and the like, we do not wish to imply that this influence is always exercised with the same degree of consciousness. In much of our reading we recognize, more or less instinctively, that the book we are dealing with belongs to this category and not another, without fully realizing how much our expectations as readers are conditioned by the conventions governing that category. It would be an entirely different matter, however, if the author were without warning to violate those conventions. If, for example, the detective in a 'whodunit' were to turn out to be the perpetrator of the crime, our natural reaction would be to exclaim, 'What sort of detective story is this?' In the same way, we would be made sharply aware of the conventions of apocalyptic if, to use John Barton's example, we were to read these words: 'But in those days, after that tribulation, the sun will be darkened and the moon will not give its light, and the stars will be falling from heaven, and the powers in the heavens will be shaken'; and then, immediately afterwards, these: 'The rest of the country will have sunny intervals and scattered showers.'[2]

What is true of readers is no doubt true of writers too. It is clear that contemporary writers differ enormously in the degree to which they are conscious of following literary conventions in the moment of composition. On the one hand, anyone composing a Petrarchan sonnet could hardly fail to be acutely conscious of the form they were following. In the same way, anyone who deviates from a conventional literary form or actually creates a new form can hardly fail to be conscious of being an innovator. On the other hand, with some writers the process of composition begins with them seeing pictures in their head.[3] If this is true of contemporary writers, who are sometimes able to describe the process of composition in retrospect, there is no reason to think that it has not always been so. However, the fact that writers do vary in the degree to which they are consciously influenced by literary conventions does not affect the fact that they are so influenced and that different writings do exhibit a family resemblance and can appropriately be classified as belonging to the same genre.

But, and this is one of the main points I wish to make in this chapter, as the form in which the writer has expressed himself varies, so should the manner in which one handles what he has written. This point can best be illustrated by comparing three of the commonest forms of discourse in the New Testament, viz. argument, narrative and parable. It should be clear that this is not an attempt to give an exhaustive account of the different genres and styles within the New Testament. A full account would have to include sayings, hymns, confessions of faith, doxologies, prophetic oracles, thanksgivings and others as well. Here is a dictionary definition of an argument: 'a connected series of statements intended to establish a position'. This definition is incomplete, however, insofar as it leaves out of account both the arguer and the readers to whom the argument is directed – factors which are of particular importance. The first question we need to ask in the exegesis of a passage of argument is, 'Who is trying to convince whom?' We need to delineate as clearly as possible both the sender and the recipients and their respective standpoints. Having done that, we need to ask 'What is it of which the author is trying to convince his readers? What is the position which he is trying to establish?' The next step is to ascertain how he has gone about it, that is, how each statement that he makes advances the argument. A passage of argument is like a chain; scrutinizing an argument entails scrutinizing the links of which it is made up. It follows that the grammatical features to which one will need to give special attention will include the interplay of personal pronouns, the logical articulations of the text and the principal verbs, as the main bearers of the argument.

Much of Paul's letters, as well as the other letters in the New Testament, consists of argument. Something that is characteristic of the method of argument used by him and the other letter writers is the frequency with which they appeal to the Old Testament. It is all too easy to dismiss these citations as passages which may have carried some weight with the original readers but contribute nothing to the development of the argument and therefore do not merit careful attention. That would be a great mistake. The quotations in the letters are consistently used to advance the argument. They form important links in the chain.

To illustrate these points, we shall examine a passage from a letter not regarded by scholars as the work of Paul, viz. the letter to the Hebrews. The passage is 2.5–9. First of all, what is the author trying to establish? What is he trying to prove? He begins by stating in verse 5 that it is not to angels that God has subjected the world to come. If not to angels, to whom? In verses 6, 7 and 8 the author quotes Psalm 8, which speaks of God having crowned mankind with glory and honour and having put all things in subjection under his feet. Is it therefore his intention simply to assert that God has subjected the world to come not to angels but to mankind? So far it might seem so. In verse 8b, however, the argument takes a new turn, when the author asserts that we do not yet see all things subject to mankind. What we do see, and see crowned with glory and honour, is Jesus. It would appear therefore that in this passage the author is not simply making an affirmation about the destiny of mankind to rule the world under God; he is also making an affirmation about Jesus. That the latter represents at least part of his intention is also suggested by the previous chapter, in which he has appealed to the scriptures seven times over to demonstrate the superiority of the Son to the angels. But, if so, what is the connection between these two affirmations? Let us look again at the quotation from Psalm 8.4–6, introduced in verses 6–8. How does this quotation advance the argument? In their original setting, these words do affirm the destiny of mankind to rule the world, the expression 'Son of Man' in the latter part of verse 4 of the psalm being simply a synonym for 'Man'. But when we read these words again in the light of the christological thrust of the subsequent verses, they begin to shine in a new light. Anyone familiar with the Gospels knows that in each Gospel the phrase 'Son of Man' is consistently used to refer to Jesus. So it would seem that the author is already thinking of Jesus when he introduces the quotation in verse 6. Could it be then that he is solely concerned with Jesus, solely concerned to affirm that Psalm 8 is fulfilled in him? That would be difficult to maintain, in view of the opening words of the quotation, 'What is man?' He must be maintaining both something about mankind and its destiny and something about Jesus. But what is the connection? Let us look again at one of the links in the chain, the link between verse 8 and verse 9. It is surely significant that the author does not say, 'We do not see everything in subjection to him (i.e. mankind) but we see Jesus' but rather, 'We do not *yet* see everything in subjection to him but we see Jesus'. So all things are not yet subject to mankind – not yet but they will be. We are being led unmistakably towards the notion of Jesus as the representative man. To rule the world under God is mankind's destiny. We do not yet see it fulfilled. What we do see is Jesus. In him the destiny of mankind is indeed fulfilled and fulfilled *for us*. What is already true of him will one day be true also of us.

That this interpretation is correct is confirmed by two further observations. At the end of verse 9 the author adds that this Jesus whom we see crowned with glory and honour because of the suffering of death has, by the grace of God, tasted death for every one. More importantly, however, in verse 10 the author describes Jesus as 'the pioneer of their salvation'. The actual Greek word used here is *archēgos*, which is a highly significant word. At its simplest, it means 'head' or 'chief' but it is also used to mean 'founder' or 'originator'. In this sense, it is used of the founder of a city or a family or a philosophical school. One basic idea clings to the word through all these uses: an *archēgos* is someone who begins something in order that others may enter into it. He founds a city, in order that others may some day live in it. He begins a family, so that some day others may be born into it.

He founds a philosophical school, so that others may follow him into the truth. An *archēgos* therefore is one who blazes a trail for others to follow. In 12.1–2, where Jesus is again described as *archēgos*, this time as the *archēgos* of our faith, the representative nature of his achievement is even clearer. What he does, he does for us, so that we may enter into the fruits of it. Where he goes, he goes for us, in order to blaze a trail for us to follow. What he is, he is for us, so that we may become what he is.

Let us now look again at our first attempt at a statement of the author's intention, viz. to assert that God has subjected the world to come not to angels but to mankind. It is now clear that, while not completely wrong, it is inadequate. The author is asserting that God has subjected the world to come to mankind, not to angels, but also freely acknowledges that as yet this destiny has not been fulfilled. What we do see, however, is Jesus. In him we do see the destiny of mankind fulfilled and fulfilled not only in him but for mankind through him.

One letter of Paul's which is largely argumentative in its texture is II Corinthians. Many scholars believe that this letter, as it now stands, does not represent a single letter of Paul's but is made up of a number of fragments of letters, written under different conditions and at different times. However, that does not affect the fact that behind II Corinthians, as we now have it, we can detect opponents who have intruded themselves into the Corinthian church and attacked both Paul's person and his ministry, thus compelling him to write to the Corinthians in the way he has.

These opponents seem to be a different group from those whom Paul encountered in Galatia,[4] since they show no interest in circumcision, the keeping of the Sabbath or cultic purity, yet they also appear to have been Jews, and Jews who prided themselves on their Jewishness, since a main theme of II Corinthians 11 is that Paul is as good a Jew as any of his opponents.

Paul refers to these opponents sarcastically as 'sham apostles', who were masquerading as apostles of Christ (11.4–15). They had evidently slandered his courage (10.1) and his apostolic authority (10.8), partly on the grounds that he had taken no money (11.7). They had also ridiculed him as having no presence and being a contemptible speaker (10.10; cf. 11.6). In addition, they may well have asserted their superiority to Paul on the grounds of having had some contact with the historical Jesus (cf. II Cor. 5.16). According to Paul, these men were trying to introduce their own version of Christianity to Corinth (11.4) and to introduce themselves as the spiritual lords and masters of the community (11.13, 20), and not without success.

One means by which they established themselves at Corinth was by the use of letters of recommendation from recognized authorities (3.1), which probably chronicled their deeds of spiritual power.

In 5.12f. Paul also accuses them of boasting 'in appearance and not in heart' (C. K. Barrett's translation), a phrase which evidently refers to external things as against inner reality and suggests superficially impressive achievements.

In the light of all this, it is significant that in another passage, 4.5, Paul declares, 'We preach not ourselves.' It seems that his opponents were guilty of just that, of not simply boasting of themselves but of preaching themselves, of parading the visible evidence of their possession of the Spirit and flaunting their superiority to Paul in personal presence.[5]

This is one of many passages which acquire a sharp polemical point when read against the background of what we know about Paul's opponents. Another is Paul's declaration in II Cor. 12.5 that he will boast of nothing but his weaknesses. It was of their strengths that his opponents boasted, of their deeds of spiritual power. Paul knows that God's power is made perfect in weakness.

Paul's reference in II Cor. 4.10 to the life of Jesus being manifested in our bodies is also likely to have a polemical point which is not immediately apparent. Paul's opponents in this letter have often been taken to be dualistic spiritualists, but the evidence we have reviewed does not support that theory. What they do appear to have questioned was whether the body of someone like Paul could serve as such a place of revelation, this Paul, who was so unimpressive in personal presence and had suffered so much hardship and persecution. Paul's response is to insist that the life of Jesus can be truly manifested in us only if we are continually carrying about in our very body the dying of Jesus, only if we are continually being handed over to death for Jesus's sake (v.11). Thus he opposes their theology of glory by his theology of the cross.

In this letter therefore Paul is trying to bridge a widening gulf, and the full force of what he is saying can only be appreciated when one perceives how wide that gulf is.

The situation which Paul confronts in I Corinthians is similar but with one significant difference. Here too, Paul is trying to bridge a widening gap. Here too, he is seeking to correct misconceptions. The difference is that there is no evidence at this stage of the presence of intruders in the Corinthian church who have slandered both Paul's apostleship and his gospel. At most, Paul has been the object of some criticism for his refusal to accept payment as an apostle (9.1ff.). The fact that the church had written to Paul seeking his advice (7.1) shows that he retained his authority in their eyes. The gap, however, between where the Corinthians are and where Paul would wish them to be has become considerable, so that Paul has to address a whole array of apparently independent problems. At the root of them all, however, we can detect one fundamental misconception, viz. that they were already blessed with everything God had to give, and, in particular, with a superior wisdom not vouchsafed to ordinary believers.[6] Our concern at the moment is not to give an exhaustive account of their erroneous notions but to show how the full force of what Paul has to say on any issue can only be perceived when one discerns where the Corinthians themselves stood.

One of the many issues Paul takes up with them is that of the gifts of the Spirit. What the Corinthians believed about the gifts of the Spirit can be reconstructed with a fair measure of confidence as follows.

First, by the gifts of the Spirit the Corinthians meant something given to them for their own enrichment, their personal benefit. Theirs was a community which was conspicuously deficient in a sense of mutual responsibility. They were torn apart by competing factions (chs. 1–4). They were taking one another to court (ch. 6). They delighted in parading their Christian freedom, reckless of the effect it might have on weaker brethren (ch. 8). They were failing to wait for latecomers at the eucharistic meal (11.17–34). And yet they had the Spirit. Clearly, for them the Spirit had nothing to do with 'my neighbour'; it only had to do with me, my enrichment.

Secondly, by the gifts of the Spirit, the Corinthians meant something abnormal, spectacular, 'out of this world', especially the gift of speaking in tongues. The care and tact with which Paul disparages the over-evaluation of tongue-speaking in ch. 14 shows unmistakably how highly the Corinthians must have regarded it.

Thirdly, the Corinthians saw the gifts of the Spirit as the possession of a privileged few, a spiritual élite. We have already found reason to think that they set great store by speaking in tongues. At the same time, Paul's question in 12.30, 'Do all speak with tongues?' clearly expects the answer, 'No'. If not all had this gift, then those who did must have been seen as especially favoured.

It is only when one discerns these beliefs in the background that one can fully appreciate the sharpness of Paul's critique. For, in contrast to the first assumption of the Corinthians, Paul affirms that the way in which the Spirit manifests its presence is by endowing the believer with the capacity to perform a specific service for the good of the church. In contrast to the second assumption of the Corinthians, Paul makes it plain that the gifts of the Spirit need in no way be striking, spectacular or 'out of this world'. Side by side with the apostolate and the working of miracles, Paul lists things that it would never have entered the Corinthians' heads to regard as the effect of the Spirit, such as helpful deeds and services of administration. In contrast to their third assumption, Paul affirms that God gives his Spirit, the gift of his grace, to every believer (I Cor. 12.7,11; cf. Rom. 12.3; I Cor. 3.5).

We have discussed I and II Corinthians, but what about Romans? As we saw in the previous chapter, the occasion of Romans is a complex one, in so far as the letter is occasioned not only by the situation of the people Paul is addressing but also by the situation in which Paul finds himself. In form, however, Romans is as argumentative a letter as any of the others, with a particular opponent kept constantly in view. That opponent is a representative of those Jews who have so often, in synagogue or market place, objected to the gospel Paul was preaching. Indeed, this imaginary interlocutor plays an active role in the whole process of composition. Again and again a new train of thought appears to be triggered off by Paul's anticipation of an objection by a typical Jewish opponent.

For example, in 3.1 Paul seems to hear the objection, 'On your argument the Jew has no advantage'; at 3.31, 'You are using faith to undermine the Law'; and again at 4.1, 'But what about Abraham? Surely the story of Abraham contradicts all you have been saying?' After 5.19 he anticipates the objection, 'What then is the place of the Law?' In 6.1 Paul anticipates an objector picking up what he has just said in 5.20. 'If it is true, as you say, that where sin increased, grace abounded all the more, doesn't it become our duty to sin so as to call forth all the more grace? Doesn't sin then become a meritorious work, and isn't that the repudiation of all ethics?' The same objection has been foreshadowed in 3.7–8 and is repeated in 6.15. In 7.7 Paul anticipates once more the objection, 'What then is the place of the Law?' and repeats it again in 7.13.

After the end of chapter 8 Paul appears to hear in his mind an objection more forceful than any he has so far anticipated, 'You are a renegade Jew!' This assumption would explain the force and power of Paul's protestation in 9.1ff. of his unceasing anguish over his kinsmen by race.

The Exegesis of Narrative

We have spent some time discussing the exegesis of argument and have emphasized the importance of ascertaining as precisely as possible the standpoint of both author and addressees, the conclusion towards which the author is arguing and the way in which each statement advances the argument. By way of contrast, let us now consider narrative.

I suggested earlier that an appropriate image for argument

is that of a chain. With narrative, one is dealing with something more like a series of pictures, or, more accurately, a film, since the pictures are bound together into a unity by some pattern or movement running through them. In the exegesis of narrative, therefore, while no detail can afford to be ignored (assuming that the narrative is the work of a skilful author, who makes every word tell), the primary focus of one's attention should be the impact of the sequence as a whole, the overall pattern, the movement running through the whole. Considerable interest will also attach to the actors and their roles. As for the grammatical features of the passage, the verbs will claim particular attention: their voice, mood, tense and also the precise sequence of these various aspects of the verb. Once again these points can best be illustrated by an examination of particular passages. The two which I have chosen are Mark 9.2–8 and Luke 1.26–38.

The story found in Mark 9.2–8 is traditionally known as the Transfiguration, but let us forget the traditional title for the moment and ask if there is any movement running through the story. I suggest that there is such a movement, from transfiguration to the reality of every day. For a moment the disciples see Jesus transfigured, clothed in garments which glow with heavenly radiance and in the company of two great figures from the Old Testament, Elijah and Moses, but at the end the story, so to speak, strikes itself out. It is as if a curtain were drawn, so that the disciples see nothing more, nothing but the Jesus they had known before, the Jesus who evoked unbelief as well as belief, offence as well as acclaim. 'And suddenly looking around they no longer saw anyone with them but Jesus only' (v.8). But that movement does not go unchallenged. In the light of the story as a whole, one perceives a new significance in Peter's exclamation in verse 5: 'Master, it is well that we are here, let us make three booths, one for you and one for Moses and one for Elijah.' Peter's exclamation takes on a new significance as an attempt to resist the movement from transfiguration to the reality of every day. This is for Peter a moment of luminous certainty, since Jesus has been shown beyond all question to be the coming Messiah, and Peter is seeking to have that moment prolonged. It must not pass, it must be held on to. Behind his exclamation we can detect fear, the fear that this moment will pass and leave everything as it was before.

But can all this be affirmed with confidence? Might one not agree that there is a movement running through the story, a movement from transfiguration to the reality of every day, and that the exclamation of Peter's does stand in contrast to it and yet attach a different meaning to his words? Elijah and Moses were not only great figures of the old order, they were both particularly associated with the coming new age (cf. Deut. 18.15; Mal. 4.5). In the light of these expectations, one can readily perceive a new meaning in Peter's words, viz. that the new age has arrived in its fullness. Here and now God is tabernacling with his people.

Each of these readings of the story seems to fit. Neither appears to be an arbitrary imposition. One could indeed argue that the two readings are not mutually exclusive, since one of the marks of the new age, according to the New Testament, is precisely that then we shall walk by sight not by faith (I Cor. 13.12; II Cor. 5.7). However, the fact that the story is capable of being read in either of these ways or both at once highlights an important difference between narrative and argument. Argument has a clear tendency towards unambiguity. The force of an argument is weakened by ambiguity. With narrative the opposite is true. Far from being weakened by ambiguity, its force is enriched by it.

The same ambiguity that attaches to the significance of the movement running through the story of the Transfiguration, to use its traditional title, attaches also to the question of its intended audience. As we saw earlier, argument is by its very nature an attempt to convince someone of something, so that one can always pose the question, 'Who is it whom this author is trying to convince?' To the extent that an argument is not clearly directed towards a particular reader, it must be judged an ineffective argument. But if a story like that of the Transfiguration is capable of being read in more than one way, then the question, 'For whom is this story intended?' also admits of more than one answer. If we interpret Peter's exclamation in the way we first suggested, viz. as an attempt to prolong a moment of certainty, then the natural answer to the question, 'For whom was this story first directed?' would be, 'People who are having difficulty in maintaining their faith and who are longing to have their moment of certainty prolonged.' If so, the point of the story is that this may not be. Peter did not know what he was saying (v.6). Inexorably the curtain is drawn, leaving the disciples alone with Jesus. Faith cannot be made so secure that the disciple is left with no need to venture. Faith can receive a strong impulse from those moments when we see and hear more than usual, but we cannot take such moments with us. And yet we have the voice which says, 'Listen to him', even when there is nothing more that is special to see. That word seeks to accompany us, from the cloud, from behind the curtain, the word that tells us that in this Jesus we have to do with God.

Read in this way, as addressed primarily to people longing to prolong their moment of certainty, the story strikes home and no detail is left hanging in the air. But the story can equally well be taken as directed to people who had wrongly supposed that the age to come had arrived in its fullness. On this reading, the voice from the cloud can be given a different meaning, having not so much the force of a word as distinct from a vision, but rather that of a directive to pay heed to the teaching which Jesus has just been giving his disciples on the inevitability of suffering both for himself and for them and therefore as reinforcing the point that the age of glory has not yet arrived.

The next example of narrative is Luke 1.26–38. One way of uncovering a movement or pattern in a story is to look at the verbs. In this story we find a whole string of verbs in the future tense. In verses 31–33 there are no fewer than eight of them, eight statements of what shall come to pass. 'You *will conceive* in your womb and *will bear* a son, and you *shall call* his name Jesus. He *will be* great, and *will be called* the Son of the Most High, and the Lord God *will give* to him the throne of his father David, and he *will reign* over the house of Jacob forever; and of his kingdom there *will be* no end.' When Mary expresses amazement at all this, asking, 'How can this be, since I have no relations with a man?' the angel replies with four more predictions of what will come to pass. 'The Holy Spirit *will come* upon you, and the power of the Most High *will overshadow* you. Therefore the child to be born *will be* holy, he *will be called* Son of God.'

Then, by way of confirmation of this word of promise, the angel tells Mary what the Spirit of God is already bringing to pass in the life of her kinswoman, Elizabeth. She who was called barren has conceived, and conceived in her old age. Indeed, she is already in her sixth month. Doubt not, therefore, that my word of promise to you is to be trusted. What I have said will happen will surely come to pass. For what I have spoken to you is God's word, and no word of God shall be void of power.

If we were to sum up the story to this point in a single word, we might well choose the word 'power'. Twelve times over the angel has declared what will come to pass, will surely come to pass, because it is God's word of which he is the bearer, and God's word is a word of power. But then in verse 38 there is a change in the verbal pattern. Up till now, as the angel has been speaking, we have had a whole string of verbs in the future tense. But now Mary responds and uses the form of the verb which expresses a wish or an act of consent. 'Behold, I am the handmaid of the Lord; *let it be* to me according to your word.'

God's word, therefore, is a word of power. It does not return to him void. It accomplishes that which he purposes and prospers in the thing for which he sends it. And yet it is also true that God waits, waits for men and women to consent, waits for them to say, 'Behold, I am the handmaid of the Lord; let it be to me according to your word.'

God's word will come to pass, for God is God, and yet Mary, by her willing consent, allows God to be truly God. For that reason she is the model believer, great in faith. To be sure, her faith is awakened by God's word, but God's word is no steam-roller. It depends upon our co-operation, our willingness to say, 'Let it be.' So this story, which seems at first to speak only of the power of God, also speaks of his powerlessness.

Narrative and Theology

By way of a postscript to this section, let us note that the prominence of narrative in the Bible is of theological significance. It tells us something about the faith to which the Bible bears witness.

Narrative is characteristic of the language of the historian: this happened, then that, then that. Such language stands in contrast to the characteristic speech-form of the natural sciences, which are rightly concerned to eliminate all narrative sentences and transform them into 'If – then – sentences'. Historical science, however, cannot dispense with narrative sentences, because the historical event, or the whole sum of historical events, can never be reduced to general laws. Narrative respects the underivability of the historical, its contingency and its surprising character. It is therefore theologically important that the language of the Christian faith has been, from the beginning, so closely akin to the language of history. As Hans Weder writes, the truth which is expressed in the narrative is of a different sort from that which attaches to the theorem of Pythagoras. It is truth which was not accessible to the human spirit in every place and at every time but has come to it as *potestas aliena*, as a truth mediated by the externality of history.[7]

The Exegesis of Parable

The third genre which we shall single out for special consideration is that of parable. It is a sign of the enduring vitality of the parables of Jesus that they have occasioned an enormous amount of literature, particularly in recent decades. Indeed, it is probably no exaggeration to say that there has been more written about the parables over the last twenty years than during the previous two thousand.[8] Out of all this literature, however, certain conclusions may be singled out as being of fundamental importance.

Parables represent a unique genre, but nevertheless they exhibit some affinities with both argument and narrative. In an earlier section we defined argument as discourse which is intended to convince someone of something. To the extent that it is effective, it is unambiguous and directed towards a specific circle of readers. The parables of Jesus are always argumentative in that they are intended to convince someone of something. They are anything but aimless, anything but addressed to no one in particular. On the contrary, if there is any type of literature in the Bible which merits the description, 'a word that strikes home', then it is the parables of Jesus. Jeremias may have exaggerated when he wrote that for the greater part the parables were weapons in the defence of the gospel, vindications of the gospel against its critics,[9] but he was right to the extent that the parables, in their original setting in the ministry of Jesus, appear to have all been addressed to a specific situation and designed to make a specific point, in other words intended to convince someone of something. To this extent the parables share the unambiguity of argumentative discourse. Let a few examples suffice to illustrate the point.

The message of the parable of the Unforgiving Servant in Matt. 18.23–35 is only too painfully clear, viz. that the person who has known God's forgiveness and then shows an unforgiving spirit excludes himself from the forgiveness of God. This, however, is not because God acts in the spirit of tit-for-tat, but because anyone who, having experienced the forgiveness of God, shows an unforgiving spirit towards his brother demonstrates that he must have closed his eyes to the truth of what God has done for him. Or, to put it in another way, anyone who has any inkling of what an unpayable debt of gratitude he owes to God for forgiving his own sins will be able to do no other than forgive the sins which his brother has committed against him. The essential thrust of the parable is unmistakable, so that it is perfectly proper to say of certain interpretations of the parable that they represent a distortion of it, for example, the view that the parable teaches that we merit the forgiveness of God by our own readiness to forgive.

To take another example from Matthew, the parable of the Labourers in the Vineyard in Matt. 20.1–16 is one of the clearest examples of those parables which are, in Jeremias's words, weapons in the defence of the gospel, vindications of the gospel against its critics. It clearly affirms that the goodness of God, while not arbitrary or capricious, is something bigger than our conventional ideas of what is just and proper. Therefore, anyone who demands that God's goodness conform to his own preconceived ideas of what is just and proper, still more, anyone who cannot receive anything from God's hand without keeping an eye on what God has done for his neighbour, will inevitably be offended by it.

To take a third example, the parable of the Good Samaritan in Luke 10.30–37 is clearly intended to blow open the cautious, prudential frame of mind which is always asking, 'Where does my duty to my neighbour stop?' and to inspire the reader with the resolve to show oneself a neighbour to anyone in need.

I have been trying to show that the parables of Jesus are akin to argument in the sense that they are in their original setting attempts to convince someone of something and therefore to that extent unambiguous. But at the same time the parables are stories. Now I argued in an earlier section that effective stories lend themselves to different readings. Far from being weakened by ambiguity, their force is enriched by it. A similar thing can be said about parables. Precisely because they are stories, they are too rich for their meaning to be reduced without remainder to a single sentence. However confident one may be that one has caught the main thrust of a parable, one is always left with the feeling that something of the parable's richness has been lost. The reader may well have experienced that feeling already, in reading my own attempts to state the point of three parables on the previous pages. For example, something that is also implicit in the parable of the Good Samaritan is a recognition of the superficial advantages of a way of life less demanding than that exemplified by the Good Samaritan.

To put it in less abstract terms, there is something to be said for behaving in the way that the priest and the Levite did. You will not be guilty of any obvious offence. After all, the priest and the Levite did not beat the man up. They did not *do* anything at all. They just passed by on the other side. What is more, by behaving as the priest and the Levite did, you get to Jericho much quicker. It takes time to be a Good Samaritan, as well as money. While the Samaritan is getting off his donkey and binding up the man's wounds, the priest and the Levite are forging ahead to Jericho or Jerusalem or wherever it is that they are bound for.

One scholar who has attempted to do justice to the richness of the parables is Pierre Grelot. He has suggested that the meaning of the parable of the Prodigal Son can be enriched if one reads it three times, once from the perspective of each of its three main characters. Read from the perspective of the father, the parable teaches that even as the father offered reconciliation to his sons, so God offers us forgiveness of our sins. Read from the perspective of the prodigal son, it teaches us that as the prodigal received reconciliation when he came home and repented so will we be forgiven when we confess our sins and turn to God for forgiveness. Read from the perspective of the older brother, it teaches that we who are righteous should be glad that God extends his grace to others as well, even to the most undeserving.[10] Grelot's intention is laudable, but how flat and uninspiring are his attempts to state the point of the parable, compared to the richness of the parable itself!

I have been arguing that because the parables are stories they are too rich for their meaning to be reduced without remainder to a single sentence. This conclusion is reinforced when we consider what it is that is distinctive about parables. I have suggested that parables share the characteristics of both argumentative discourse and of stories. But it would not be adequate to define parables simply as stories with a persuasive purpose. Such a definition leaves out the element of comparison, which is an essential component of any parable.

Basic to a great deal of recent research is the thesis that parables and metaphors are analogous speech phenomena or that parables are extended metaphors and that a new understanding of the nature of metaphor which has been gaining ground more and more over the last century ought to be applied to parables also. As representative of this approach to the parables I cite the work of the American scholars Wilder, Funk, Via, Crossan, Perrin, McFague, Tolbert and Perkins and, from the Continent, the work of Fuchs, Ricoeur and Weder. To appreciate the full force of this new approach, however, one needs some understanding of the older understanding of metaphor which, in essence, goes back to Aristotle. According to that traditional understanding, metaphor is a kind of unreal speech, that is, a deviation from the use of words in their real (i.e. literal) meaning. Furthermore it is fundamentally translatable, a pictorial way of saying what could be said in some other, more direct way, a kind of ornamental accessory for which one could substitute plain language without loss of meaning.

Until fairly recently similar assumptions were commonly made, and still are widely made, about parables. On this view, parables are essentially translatable. The task of the biblical interpreter or preacher, therefore, is to state the point of the parable, to translate the story into conceptual terms. If the question is raised, why then did Jesus use them in the first place? the answer commonly given is that they were an educational tool. Jesus chose to speak in parables in order to make truths clear to people of limited capacity or to help people to see old truths in a new light. Their use, in short, was necessitated by the hearers' want of comprehension or perception.

Over recent decades, however, this understanding of metaphors and, consequently, of parables also has been more and more called in question. According to the newer understanding, anyone like a poet who creates a metaphor is not embellishing an old perception but rather making possible a new one. We resort to metaphor, in other words, in order to say something about things we know little about. As Mc Fague puts it, 'Poetic metaphor is used not as an embellishment of what can be said in some other way but precisely because what is being said is new and cannot be said any other way'.[11] Ask a critic what a poetic metaphor means and in the end he or she will be reduced to repeating the line of poetry or even the entire poem, for want of any other way of saying what is being said except in the words that were chosen to say it.

Metaphor therefore should not be regarded as unreal speech but as a special form of real speech, a form, moreover, which has a peculiar precision. 'Metaphor', writes McFague, 'is the poet's attempt to be precise and clear about something.'[12]

The reason for the ultimate untranslatability of metaphors should become clearer if we reflect further on how metaphors work. A metaphor brings into relationship two horizons of meaning represented by two words. On the face of it, the two horizons are quite different. A person is quite unlike a wire connected to a battery. Warfare is quite unlike a parlour game. Yet the metaphorical form affirms their identity. 'Liz is a live wire.' 'War is a chess game.' The affirmation of identity teases the reader or hearer into discovering what it is that the two things have in common. The metaphor lives, if it lives, out of the tension between the obvious difference and the affirmed similarity between the subject and the complement. I say 'if it lives' because living metaphors are continually becoming moribund and finally dead metaphors, as the users of a language become accustomed to them and lose any feeling for the incongruity of the original equation. On the other hand, through the creation of new metaphors the language is continually being enriched. The main point, however, is that because of the essential incongruity of the two horizons of meaning which are brought into relationship a metaphor cannot be translated into non-metaphorical terms without losing some of its meaning. The truth which comes to expression in metaphorical language cannot be fully expressed other than pictorially.

Many recent writers in this field state their conclusions more categorically than I have just done. McFague writes that 'there is no way *around* the metaphor to what is "really" being said' and that 'metaphor and symbol ought not to be manipulated, translated, reduced but contemplated, probed, reflected upon'.[13] Weder writes that a metaphorical utterance cannot be translated into real speech without losing its meaning.[14] I find the last statement a slight over-statement. Take for example, the metaphor, 'Liz is a live wire'. Now suppose that we substitute for it a prosaic statement: 'Liz is a lively person'? 'Liz is full of ideas'? Certainly neither of these statements exhausts the meaning of the metaphor, yet they are surely pointing us towards a correct understanding of it.

Douglas Berggren, however, does not lay himself open to the charge of over-statement when he writes that it is 'ultimately impossible to reduce completely the cognitive import of any vital metaphor to any set of univocal, literal or non-tensional statements'.[15]

To proceed, however, with our exposition of recent theory: if parables are understood as extended metaphors and if metaphors are considered to be ultimately untranslatable, it is only to be expected that the same thing is held to be true of parables. Parables, we are told, are not to be regarded as merely pictures of something which could be expressed equally well in literal language. The parable does not merely say something old in a new way or something true in a pictorial way; the truth that comes to expression in a parable cannot be expressed other than pictorially. This takes the ground from under every theory according to which Jesus taught in parables for the sake of his hearers. The truth which comes to expression in the parables, the truth about the kingdom of God, itself demands this form.

How, then, are the parables to be interpreted at all? The interpreter, writes Weder, must renounce the temptation to replace the parables by some statement of theological principles derived from them and instead put the parable itself in the foreground and seek to enhance its force as a story by illuminating its structure and using paraphrase.[16] In the same way McFague writes that the first thing to do with a parable is to read it, several times, work out the relations of those involved, highlight the subtleties of the story, in other words, let the story penetrate *us* rather than look around for possible interpretations of it.[17] Again I find an element of over-statement in these conclusions, insofar as they seem to do less than justice to the argumentative aspect of parables, about which I spoke earlier, but the main point must be conceded. I would hope that the attempts I have made in the previous pages to express the meaning of certain parables will be seen as pointing the reader towards a correct understanding of them but I would readily concede that they fall far short of exhausting their meaning.

McFague's comments on the parable of the Prodigal Son are worth quoting in full.

One *could* paraphrase this parable in the theological assertion, 'God's love knows no bounds,' but to do that would be to miss what the parable can do for our insight into such love. For what *counts* here is not extricating an abstract concept but precisely the opposite, delving into the details of the story itself, letting the metaphor do its job. . . . It is the play of the radical images that does the job. If we want to talk about what this parable has to say about God, we must do so in terms that do not extrapolate from that moment when the father, waiting these many months, finally sees his son.[18]

In view of the measure of ambiguity which, as we have seen, attaches to parables as stories and as extended metaphors, we can appreciate afresh the sensitivity of C. H. Dodd's definition of a parable, offered over fifty years ago, as 'a metaphor or simile drawn from nature or common life, arresting the hearer by its vividness or strangeness and leaving the mind in sufficient doubt about its precise application to tease it into active thought'.[19]

It is because the meaning of the parables of Jesus is too rich to be represented without remainder by a single statement that they proved already within the New Testament period to be readily susceptible to reinterpretation. It is a widely accepted conclusion of Gospel criticism that many of the parables in the Gospels show signs of having been reapplied to meet the church's changing needs and circumstances.

It is above all to Dodd and Jeremias that we owe what understanding we have of the processes of reapplication. These two scholars detected a history of continual use and re-use of the parables. They had been expanded. They had been made to speak to new situations. Parables which were originally addressed to opponents had been treated by the early church as if they had originally been addressed to disciples, and this change in the audience had been accompanied by a change in point.[20]

In one respect, however, the conclusions of Jeremias, in particular, stand in need of qualification, viz. his unwillingness to see any value in the church's reapplications of the parables. Jeremias regarded what he had identified as later expansions and reapplications as things which had to be got rid of, in order to reach the authentic words of Jesus. On the dust cover of the first edition of his book it said: 'Like a skilful restorer of an old Master, working with loving care and searching scholarship, he has freed the parables from the dust of allegorical and hortatory interpretations and made them shine out afresh.' As if the reapplications of later Christians were only so much dust or grime!

These are the words of the publisher, not of Jeremias himself, yet they do express his intention correctly, as can be seen from the closing words of his long discussion of the return to Jesus from the primitive church.[21]

> These seven laws of transformation . . . will help us to lift in some measure here and there the veil, sometimes thin, sometimes almost impenetrable, which has fallen upon the parables of Jesus. How great the gain if we succeed in rediscovering here and there behind the veil the features of the Son of Man! To meet with him can alone give power to our preaching.

The evaluation of the process of reapplication which that statement implies is wholly negative, since the process is described as a veiling of the original meaning. Many scholars would now take the view that the early church was fully justified in reapplying the parables in the way it did and that the way in which the parables lent themselves to such reapplication is a sign of their richness and vitality.

Let us take, as an example, the parable of the Sower. If one tries to read the story setting aside the attached explanation, two things, surely, stand out. One is the severity of the setbacks which the sower meets at the outset. The other is the size of the eventual harvest. These two striking features confirm the common interpretation of the parable as one of assurance: in spite of seemingly endless setbacks there will be at the end an abundant harvest. But now let us picture a congregation of mainly Gentile Christians listening to that parable in Rome in the sixties. They could have put the emphasis where Jesus put it, on the abundant harvest at the end after all the setbacks of the beginning, but what would have happened, had they done so? How easy it would have been for them to draw the conclusion, 'Yes, by and large the Jews rejected the gospel, but we Gentiles have accepted it. And here we are!' But somewhere a teacher said to himself, 'We cannot be meant to take from this story a lesson that simply makes us complacent.' And so he looked at the story afresh and asked himself, 'Why was it that, to start with, the seed all went to waste? Because of hard ground, predatory birds, rocky soil and weeds. Why is it, then, that the preaching of the gospel so often seems to be fruitless? Because it meets with people like that, people who succumb all too easily to the temptations of other voices, people with no staying power, people who are preoccupied with the things of this world.' And so, looking at the story from a new angle, this unknown teacher found in it, without any forcing or distortion, a new point, a point which was the right word for his people, a point which he believed was Christ's word for them.

An important addition now needs to be made to the conclusions we have reached up to this point. So far we have been speaking as if the parables all formed a homogeneous group, but that is far from being true. Since Jülicher, it has become common to draw a distinction between similitudes, parables proper, illustrations and allegories. Similitudes tell of a typical situation or a typical or regular event. Many similitudes begin with the words, 'Which of you. . . ?' (Matt. 7.9; Luke 14.28; 15.4; 17.7).

Parables proper, on the other hand, consist of freely composed stories. A typical beginning of a parable proper is, 'There was a man who. . . .' (Matt. 21.28; Luke 14.16).

Illustrations are, like parables, invented stories, but they work in a different way. In a parable proper, one has to make a transference from the world of the story to the world which the storyteller is seeking to illumine by it. An illustration, on the other hand, describes someone's conduct and holds it up either for emulation (as in the story of the Good Samaritan, Luke 10.29–37) or by way of warning (as in the parable of the Rich Fool, Luke 12.16–21).

Allegory is defined in the *Oxford Dictionary* as 'description of a subject under the guise of some other subject of aptly suggestive resemblance'. That is to say, it is a story which is symbolical both as a whole and in its details. The question one has to be constantly asking oneself in reading an allegory is, 'What does this person or event or item stand for?'[22] Because the allegory is related to the world of the hearer not at one crucial point but at a whole number of points, allegories do not bring about in the hearer a radical reorientation, the 'shock of the new'. A succession of parallels cannot convey a sudden flash of insight. We have noted in the previous chapter the distortions which result when the parable of the Good Samaritan is treated, as it was consistently from Marcion to Trench, as a full-blown allegory.

One further observation about the distinctiveness of the parables of the Bible: this genre, above all other literature in the Bible, is intended to elicit a response. The biblical parables are designed to fire the imagination of the hearers, to engage them, to draw them in and lead them to a moment of insight when they see themselves in an altogether new way, a way which leads inexorably to a decision. We see this especially clearly in the parable which Nathan tells to David in II Sam. 12.1–7 about the rich man and his neighbour with one ewe lamb. By verses 5 and 6 David is so fully drawn into the story that he exclaims that the rich man deserves to die and declares that he shall be made to restore the lamb fourfold. Then in verse 7 comes the moment of insight, 'You are the man'; and finally in verse 13, decision: 'I have sinned against the Lord.'

In the same way Jesus does not tell parables simply in order to teach people about something but to do something to them. As McFague puts it, 'If the listener or reader "learns" what the parable has to "teach" him or her, it is more like a shock to the nervous system than it is like a piece of information to be stored in the head.'[23] And again: 'Those who have followed the movement of the two "logics" of the parable of the wedding feast find themselves provoked, stimulated, edged into a decision about which "logic" will be their own. . . . The parable does not teach a spectator a lesson; rather it invites and surprises a participant into an experience.'[24] In this way the hearer is given the opportunity to be brought into a relationship with the kingdom of God, a relationship which involves not only the head and the heart

but the hands and the feet. It is significant that the parable of
the Good Samaritan does not end with the words, 'Now you
know who your neighbour is', but 'Go and do thou likewise.'

A comparison can appropriately be made between a
parable and a joke. People tell jokes with the aim of doing
something to other people, moving them to laughter. Your
aim in telling a joke is only achieved when I laugh. In the
same way, Jesus's aim in telling parables is only achieved
when I respond to them. Through that response of mine the
kingdom of which the parables speak becomes a reality in my
life. The parables are not simply the linguistic tool which
Jesus chose in order to talk about the kingdom, they are the
means of its coming, the means by which it becomes a reality
in our lives. Yet the parable remains a word which draws
without compelling. We who listen are left free to respond.
We can resist, if we choose to do so.

A Concern for Particularity

The main thesis of this chapter has been that the critical
reader should always try to identify the genre of the passage
which he or she is studying. For, as the genre of the passage
varies, so should the manner in which one handles it.
Throughout I have been stressing the importance of the
reader acquiring a feel for what this piece of writing has in
common with other writings, in other words, for its genre,
and, furthermore, of adopting a method of interpretation
appropriate to that genre. But this concern needs to be
balanced by a concern for particularity.

For example, while recognizing that there are passages in
the Gospels which can properly be described as allegory, we
need to be careful not to assume that they exhibit all the
features of allegories elsewhere. It was this assumption
which led Jülicher and many scholars after him to draw
unduly sweeping conclusions about the historicity of the
allegories in the Gospels. Jülicher observed that allegories in
general exhibit a pronounced tendency to unreality, considered as stories. Stones can move of their own volition, eagles
plant vines, beasts have wings, stars become bulls. If we ask
why this is so, the answer must be that it is extraordinarily

difficult to write a story which is both a picture of a whole set of spiritual facts and a convincing, life-like story. At the same time, to accept such unrealistic details does not present great difficulties to the reader, who is all the time conscious of the spiritual world of which the story is a symbol. An allegory, as has often been said, is a kind of description in code. The question which the reader of an allegory is constantly asking is, 'What does this person or event or feature of this story stand for?' It is because one's attention is focussed on the world symbolized by the story that one can accept without difficulty a measure of unreality in the story *qua* story. In view of this tendency of allegories, *qua* stories, to exhibit a tendency to unreality, it is understandable that Jülicher took over from traditional rhetoric the designation of allegory as unreal speech. But, having reached that conclusion, it was almost inevitable that he should go on to dismiss the allegories found in the Gospels as the work of the early church. How could unreal speech be the work of Jesus himself? Yet the conclusion was premature. It is, to be sure, extraordinarily difficult to compose a story which both serves to symbolize a whole set of spiritual facts and conveys an impression of reality, but might not a supreme artist succeed in doing just that? May not the parable of the Wicked Husbandman in Mark 12.1–12 represent such a story? If so, on what grounds could one describe this parable, for all its allegorical features, as an example of unreal speech? The question of its authenticity, that is, the question whether it is or is not the work of the historical Jesus, is of course a complex one and involves other considerations.[25]

As with allegory, so with parable. The whole body of the parables of Jesus, and not just those which exhibit allegorical features, have distinctive characteristics. We noted earlier that through metaphor the language is continually being enriched. The network of conventional meanings is burst, the dominant speech tradition broken open. This has its counterpart in the parables in the way in which the familiar world is changed. Again and again as one reads the parables of Jesus, one is brought up short – by an unexpected turn in the narrative or by an element of extravagance which, while not actually impossible, nevertheless represents the extreme limits of the possible. Amos Wilder speaks of 'that certain shock to the imagination' which the parables provide.[26] Thus the behaviour of the householder in the parable of the labourers in the Vineyard in Matthew 20 seems to fly in the face both of strict justice and sound economics. The servant in the parable of the Unmerciful Servant in Matt. 18.23–35 is represented as owing a colossal sum, amounting to fifty times as much as the yearly tribute of Galilee and Peraea in 4 BC.[27] Again it is quite extraordinary that all those who had been invited to a feast should rudely refuse the invitation of the host, so compelling him to send out invitations to everybody at random, the bad and the good (Matt. 22.9–10). Or again what landlord would let his tenants treat his servants shamefully and simply keep sending others and finally his son (Mark 12.1–12)?

All this is due, we may add, to the worldly being brought into a predicative relationship to God. The new meaning which the subject of the narrative acquires through being predicated metaphorically of the kingdom of God leaves its traces behind in the narrative structure itself. As in the incarnation itself so in the literary form of the parable, the central form of Jesus's teaching, 'the transcendent comes to ordinary reality and disrupts it'.[28]

In the same way, while it is true that all of the acknowledged writings of Paul can rightly be described as letters, as distinct from literary epistles,[29] that is, real letters to a specific reader or circle of readers, we must also recognize that, as Günther Bornkamm says, they also link up with entirely different forms, those of the sermon, of theological argumentation, of exhortation, and of the liturgy (confessions, hymns, doxologies, blessings and cursings and so on): and that these elements give them a theological weight which sets them apart from any letters written before his time and made them hard for even his ardent admirers to emulate after his time.[30]

Moreover, one must always bear in mind the possibility that while a writer may be consciously following an accepted literary form, he may in certain respects be deliberately deviating from it. I emphasized at the beginning of the chapter the extent to which we are influenced, often unconsciously, by the conventions governing a particular literary genre, and the confusion that would be caused in the reader's mind if an author were, without warning, to violate those conventions, for example, by having the detective turn out to be the perpetrator of the crime. However, the introduction of a slight deviation from the conventional pattern can give an extremely effective twist to a detective story.

Agatha Christie has done this very skilfully in *The Man In The Brown Suit*. In this novel she adopts the device of having the central character, Anne Beddingfeld, relate the story in the first person. In the second paragraph of the first chapter, Anne Beddingfeld acknowledges having filled in the gaps in her own knowledge by recourse to Sir Eustace Pedler's diary, of which he had kindly begged her to make use. Sir Eustace Pedler plays a prominent part in the story as it unfolds, and a number of chapters, eight in all out of a total of thirty-six, consist simply of extracts from his diary. Sir Eustace thus almost becomes a co-author of the story. It comes therefore as quite a shock to the reader to discover in the last chapter that he is in fact the criminal. This book is an interesting example of an author giving a novel twist to the conventions of the genre without actually subverting them.

The critical reader of the Bible also needs to be on the lookout for deliberate deviations from conventional literary patterns. A good example is provided by the story of the annunciation in Luke 1.26–38. This is one of several stories of annunciation in the Bible and these stories exhibit enough of a common pattern to constitute them a minor genre. Luke's story contains several of the common elements but also has some features that are unique. For example, in other annunciation stories in the Bible the response to the message often takes the form of an objection or a request for a sign. Mary does neither. She is content to ask the simple question, 'How can this be?' and, having received an answer, to declare her readiness to be God's instrument.

Such deviations can be of considerable theological significance. Some scholars have expended a great deal of energy on trying to fit the stories of the resurrection appearances into conventional literary patterns, whether they be theophany, angelophany, the appearance of a spirit

from Sheol or whatever, but the stories stubbornly resist
being reduced to any familiar narrative type from the Jewish
or Hellenistic repertoire. Central to the Easter stories, for
example, is the concern to establish the identity of the one
who appears with the one who had recently been crucified
and to show this 'having-been-crucified-one' as continuing
his ministry under new conditions and on a wider scale.[31]

This concern creates a story with a new pattern. Thus the
very irregularity of these stories testifies to the newness of
what lies behind them. As Rowan Williams observes, the
stories are irregular and unconventional, we may assume,
because what lay behind them was unexpected and bewilder-
ing. Something radically fresh in speech and narrative has
been generated by something new – the resurrection
encounter.[32]

The main thesis of the last part of this chapter is that the
critical reader needs to be alert to the particularity and
uniqueness of the biblical writings. I have spoken of how
passages which appear to belong to an existing genre, such as
allegory or parable, may in fact differ subtly from earlier
prototypes; and of how an author may deliberately deviate
from a literary form which he is using as his model. But the
reader also needs to be alert to variations among books
which, on the face of it, belong to the same genre. For
example, even the use of the term 'gospel' to describe
Matthew, Mark, Luke and John is unhelpful if it has the
effect of blurring the very real differences between them. For
example, Luke exhibits much more of a biographical interest
than the other three, whereas the differences between the
first three Gospels and the fourth are such that no careful
reader of the New Testament can fail to notice them. For
instance, whereas in the Synoptic Gospels the teaching of
Jesus is made up of parables and short pregnant sayings,
which can also be detected in the longer speech complexes,
in John the teaching takes the form of long meditative
discourses which usually grow out of a preceding narrative
and revolve around only a few themes. The common use of
the word 'discourse' rather than, say, teaching or argument
to describe the speeches of Jesus in John is itself a recognition
of their uniqueness. C. H. Dodd lays his finger on what is

distinctive about John's speeches, when he compares them to musical compositions.

> Chs. ii–xii ... form an organic whole. A continuous argument runs through them. It does not move along the direct line of a logical process. Its movement is more like that of a musical fugue. A theme is introduced and the two are interwoven; then a third, and so on. A theme may be dropped, and later resumed and differently combined, in all manner of harmonious variations. The themes are those of life, light and judgement, the passion and the glory of Christ, and the like.[33]

It would be equally mistaken to suppose that all of Paul's letters were of a piece. While it may be true that the texture of much of Galatians and I and II Corinthians is of the nature of argument, the same thing can hardly be said of I Thessalonians. For the first three chapters Paul is content to recall to his readers the ministry he had recently exercised among them, to describe his movements since leaving them and to pour out his feelings towards them. Then he passes to parainesis or exhortation and, towards the end of chapter 4 (4.13) to what is better described as teaching rather than argument, since Paul is not correcting misapprehensions so much as filling in the gaps in their understanding (3.10).

I Thessalonians provides a good example of a further feature of the biblical literature to which the critical reader needs to be alert, viz. the variety of style to be found within the one writing. I stated earlier that much of the epistle to the Romans is argumentative in character. However, it would be a great mistake to assume that this were true of the whole letter or even of the more doctrinal chapters, viz. chapters 1–11. For example, the first eleven verses of chapter 5 are more doxological in tone than argumentative, a song of praise to God for the riches of his grace, a celebration of the love of God which in Christ has made our lost cause its own and with him will freely give us all it has to give. The same thing is even more true of chapter 8, especially in the final paragraphs. C. H. Dodd again captures admirably the variety of style in Romans when he writes at the beginning of his exposition of 8.18–25 as follows.

At this point the argument rises to a new level. We have heard Paul declaiming against the vices of the age like a satirist, speculating on the knowledge of God and the conscience of man like a philosopher, arguing from Scripture like a rabbi and analysing experience like a psychologist. Now he speaks with the vision of a poet.[34]

It is significant that neither chapter 5 nor chapter 8 of Romans is introduced by the anticipation of an objection, a device which, as we saw earlier, again and again triggers off a passage of argument.

Enough has been said to illustrate the need for constant alertness to the distinctiveness of each book, each passage, which one is reading. Indeed, the more I study biblical literature, the more sympathy I feel with a remark of the English literary critic, David Daiches,

> The more I read and think about and talk about literature, the more dubious I become of fixed categories and text-book definitions and the more important it seems to me to expose oneself to the reality and variety of literary works themselves.[35]

To say this, however, is not to deny the value of classification according to genre, of searching for what a book or passage has in common with other writings, in order to apply to the book or passage one is studying insights which have proved fruitful elsewhere. What the critical reader needs constantly to aim at is a feel for this writing both in its similarity to other writings and in its distinctiveness. That, I take it, is part of what structuralist authors have in mind when they speak of literary competence.[36]

4

The Whole and the Parts

In Chapter 2 we discussed at some length the legitimacy of
concentration on authorial intention as the primary goal of
exegesis. Our first main thesis was that the quest for
authorial intention can be held to be legitimate, in view of
the peculiarly pastoral, and therefore intentional, character
of all the New Testament writings, whatever their genre. In
arguing this thesis, however, we were, to a large extent,
concerned with the various New Testament writings as
wholes, not with particular passages. Granted, however, that
the writings as wholes are intentional and that the intentions of their various authors can be inferred with some
confidence, what about the intentionality of individual
passages? How do we set about discovering what Mark was
concerned above all to communicate to his readers, as he
wrote this story; or Paul, as he dictated this paragraph; or
John, the seer, as he related this vision?

It is my conviction that there is a dialectical relationship
between one's understanding of a particular passage and
one's understanding of a book as a whole. At this moment I
may be attempting an exegesis of this passage but, as a
student of the New Testament, I am also seeking to form an
overall judgment about this work as a whole and about this
writer. These two aims are complementary and interdepen-
dent. The wider my knowledge of particular passages, the
greater will be my capacity to understand the work as a
whole and its author; conversely, the richer my understanding of the work as a whole and its author, the more I will be
able to see in a particular passage.

Where to Start?

Granted, however, that these two pursuits are mutually enriching, the question still arises, where is the best starting-point? With the particular passage or with the total work? With the parts or the whole? The main contention in this chapter is that the best starting-point is with the whole. The best way to attain to a coherent interpretation of a passage is to work consistently from the whole to the parts and back again to the whole. That is to say, I move from what I know of this book as a whole to this particular passage; from what I can discern about this passage as a whole to this particular verse; from what I can perceive to be the point of this verse as a whole to its components. But this closer and closer attention to detail should be accompanied by a continual questioning of my provisional understanding of the larger wholes. We thus see afresh the importance of the rule enunciated in Chapter 2 that we should be continually testing any provisional understanding we may have of an author's intent in any passage by what he has actually said and left unsaid.

It is always tempting, when beginning an exegesis, to dive into commentaries and accumulate as much information as possible about the details of the passage, details of text and grammar and historical allusion and the like. Moreover, the way in which some commentaries are set out encourages such a procedure. Some commentaries, for example, those in the International Critical Commentary series, largely consist of a series of learned footnotes on individual words and phrases. Raymond Brown, in his Anchor Bible commentaries on John and the Johannine Epistles, provides the reader with two kinds of exegesis. The one kind, which he calls *Notes*, contains learned footnotes in the style of the ICC series. The other kind, which he calls *Comment*, offers an interpretation of the meaning of the passage as a whole. The Notes, however, precede the Comment. In his commentary on Luke in the same series, Joseph Fitzmyer retains the distinction between Notes and Comment but reverses the order. If the main contention of this chapter is sound, Fitzmyer's order is the better of the two. For one thing, if one begins by combing

the commentaries for detailed information, there is a real
danger that one will be swamped by what has been not
unfairly called a 'pedantic dust-storm' and simply fail to see
the wood for the trees. There is also the danger that one will
get sidetracked by details which are quite peripheral to the
meaning of the passage as a whole or that one will persist in
entertaining some concept of its total meaning which is, in
fact, mistaken. The last point calls for some elaboration.

Beginning with the Whole

In reading the Bible, I am not reading a strange book but one
which I hear read and expounded regularly in church and
with which I have been familiar for decades. From all this
previous experience I already have some concept of this
author and of this work of his, and therefore some idea of
what to look for in this particular passage. These expectations may not be lying in the forefront of my mind. If
they are not, I need to make them as explicit as possible.
They will be significantly clarified, however, if, before I
attempt to study a particular passage in detail, I read the
whole work right through. The point of doing this will be
seen more clearly if we recall what was said in Chapter 2 to
the effect that each one of Paul's epistles, as they are usually
called, is a genuine letter, written from this man, Paul, to this
particular community, Galatia or Philippi or whatever.
As Willi Marxsen observes in his commentary on
I Thessalonians, a letter is a literary unity. The individual
sections, still more individual verses, can therefore only
rightly be understood within the framework of the whole.
No one receiving a letter today would ever entertain the idea
of reading first of all page 3, then page 2 and then page 5. We
do not even adopt such a procedure with letters addressed to
ourselves. With letters addressed to others such a method of
reading would appear quite absurd. Therefore anyone who is
interested in a particular section or even a particular verse
from I Thessalonians only has the chance to understand it
properly if he or she first takes account of the contents of the
whole letter.[1]

Here is an example of how an acquaintance with this letter

as a whole (I Thessalonians) can preclude a misunderstand-
ing of a particular passage. For the best part of two chapters
Paul seems to be saying over and over again, 'Remember,
remember. Remember how I brought you the gospel and
conducted myself among you. Remember how you accepted
that gospel and how you have tried to live by it.' Here are
some typical verses: 'We call to mind, before our God and
Father, how your faith has shown itself in action, your love in
labour and your hope of our Lord Jesus Christ in fortitude'
(1.3, NEB). 'When we brought you the gospel, we brought it
not in mere words but in the power of the Holy Spirit and
with strong conviction, as you know well' (1.5, NEB). 'This is
why we thank God continually, because when we handed on
God's message, you received it, not as the word of men but as
what it truly is, the very word of God at work in you who hold
the faith' (2.13, NEB).

What is the point of all this? Is Paul defending himself
against attacks which have been made upon him during his
absence? If we confine our attention to these passages alone,
that may well seem to be a reasonable assumption. It may
well seem the more reasonable, when we recall other letters
of Paul's such as Galatians or II Corinthians. In those letters
he is concerned to defend himself against the slanders of
opponents who were trying to undo his work. But, when we
look at I Thessalonians as a whole, we find no evidence that
anyone has been slandering Paul in Thessalonica or trying to
undo his work. On the contrary, he is able to say to them, 'I
am told that you always think kindly of us and are as anxious
to see us as we are to see you' (3.6).

We must, therefore, look in another direction for an
explanation of why Paul spends so much time saying to his
readers, 'Remember, remember'. Once again a perusal of the
letter as a whole proves useful, for it reveals that, since Paul
left their city, the Thessalonians had had to endure persecution from their fellow citizens, something which they
evidently did not really expect. Moreover, some of their
members have died, and it is clear that they had not been
prepared for this to happen before the Lord's return. Paul's
purpose, therefore, in saying to them over and over again,
'Remember, remember', would seem to have been to deal

with any doubts they may have had about their first experience with the gospel. 'Yes,' he is saying, 'the message we brought you was for real, the very word of God himself.'

I have been arguing that our previous knowledge of a writing and its author should be sufficient to provide us with some idea of his main concerns, and therefore of what to look out for in a particular passage, and that these expectations will be significantly clarified (and the likelihood of our being misled by false clues significantly lessened), if, before we attempt to study any passage in detail, we read the whole work right through. Our surmises about what is the author's intent in this particular passage will be clarified still further, if we now take the further step of re-reading the passage right through. By allowing the passage as a whole to make its impact upon us, we ought to be able to form a provisional concept of what it is all about.

Yet it can be no more than a provisional concept. We must now begin to move from the passage as a whole to its component parts. As was indicated in the previous chapter, we must examine its structure: the various steps in the argument, if it is argumentative in character; its development and emphasis, if it is a story or a parable. If our exegesis is not to crumble up into a lot of observations of detail, it is essential that we should penetrate the texture of the text and become aware of its internal organization and movement. Having done that, we must go on to examine in detail the various verses or groups of verses of which it is composed. Here we shall be well-advised to follow the same procedure, viz. to attempt first of all to grasp the meaning of the unit as a whole and then move to the examination of its details, the words, the expressions, the concepts which make up the threads of the fabric.

In examining the passage in greater and greater detail, however, our aim remains that of clarifying our understanding of the meaning of the passage as a whole, so that we can return at the end to our provisional formulation of what the passage is all about and ask ourselves how far it has been confirmed and how far enlarged or modified or corrected. The direction of the movement of our enquiry should be from the whole to the parts and back again to the whole.

In German theological faculties and seminaries students are usually expected to conclude an exegetical exercise with what is called the *skopus*. This is the Latin form of a Greek word which denotes a mark or object on which one fixes the eye, such as the target at which an archer is aiming, and hence, by extension, an aim, end or object. As used in exegesis, the *skopus* denotes a brief statement of the author's aim in the passage in question. The point of such an exercise is to enable the student to grasp as clearly as possible the essential thrust of the passage, its controlling direction. This can be a great help towards the preparation of a sermon.

In a book written for French pastors and students Max-Alain Chevallier suggests the following *skopi* for four textual subdivisions which he identifies in I Corinthians 13:

1–3: the most extraordinary performances of piety are worthless without love.

4–7: what is love? a disposition always open to new ways of expressing itself.

8–12:let us not be mistaken, love is *the* final value.

13: love is the greatest of the values of the present time.[2]

Another passage which he examines in some detail is Luke 3.21–22. He sums up the thrust of this passage as follows:

Jesus endowed with the Spirit and proclaimed Son: an event which inaugurates his mission and establishes Christian baptism.[3]

Chevallier also recommends the student or pastor to carry the process even further and crystallize the meaning of the passage in a sequence of sub-titles plus an over-all title for the passage as a whole. As an over-all title for I Corinthians 13 he proposes: 'Love – the alpha and omega of piety.'[4]

The Hermeneutical Circle

In recommending the procedure of working from the whole to the parts and back again to the whole, I have in fact been advocating what has been known since Schleiermacher as the hermeneutical circle. It is a concept which has won very wide acceptance; different forms and applications of it appear particularly in the works of Dilthey, Heidegger, Bultmann and Gadamer.[5]

Willi Marxsen formulates the principle as follows in the foreword to his commentary on I Thessalonians. He writes:

> Exegesis must begin with the whole and from there lead to the understanding of the individual details. Here, of course, we have a circle: a more precise understanding of the detail will deepen one's understanding of the whole and can also lead to a modification of one's provisional understanding of the whole, but one always ought to step into the circle at the point of grasping the whole, even when it communicates at first merely an impression which is only more or less clear and only later acquires profile and more exact contours. The whole forms an organic unit, but that is something very different from a collection of details.[6]

Gadamer stresses particularly the provisional nature of any proleptic notion we may form of the meaning of the whole. Any person who is trying to understand a text is always performing an act of projecting. He projects before himself a meaning for the text as a whole, as soon as some initial meaning emerges in his reading of it. But this 'fore-project' is constantly revised in terms of what emerges as he penetrates into the meaning,[7] until he attains a harmony of all the details with the whole.[8] It is, however, important that we make this process as conscious as possible, if we are to be sensitive to the text's quality of newness. We need to be aware of the projections which we are in fact bringing to the text, aware of our own bias, so that we may really experience the 'shock of the new', which breaks the spell of our own fore-meanings, wherever they are inadequate.[9]

For an illustration we turn again to I Corinthians 13. The fore-meaning of this passage which we bring with us is likely to be that of a hymn, a hymn to love. But when we read the passage carefully in the light of the letter as a whole, we soon discover how inadequate such a description is. It fails altogether to bring out its polemical point. Paul is engaging here in sustained polemic, not so obviously as in I Cor. 4.6–13 but just as effectively, against the presumption of the

Corinthians to have arrived and their confusion of penulti-
mate gifts with the ultimate ones – faith, hope and love.

Verse 1 is evidently directed against an over-estimation of
tongues, verse 2 against an interpretation of prophecy as the
knowledge of mysteries, verse 3 against an over-emphasis on
the wonder-working dimensions of faith. All these gifts will
pass away, for they are inextricably part of the present
economy; love alone abides for ever (v.8). Indeed, the triad of
faith, hope and love in verse 13 may well have been
constructed in conscious opposition to a Corinthian triad of
glossolalia, prophecy and knowledge.[10]

Something that calls for especial comment is that
Schleiermacher chose to speak of a circle not a two-way
process. This is significant because the procedure he is
describing is, in fact, never-ending. The more widely I study a
particular writing in detail, the greater my capacity becomes
to understand the work as a whole, but, conversely, the fuller
my understanding of the work as a whole, the more I will be
able to see in any particular passage.

A good illustration of this latter point is afforded by Robert
Maddox in *The Purpose of Luke-Acts*. Early in that book he
discusses the preface to the Gospel of Luke in some detail. In
the last section, the last two pages in fact, he turns back to
the Gospel preface and looks at it again, in the light of his
examination (now concluded) of the whole two-volume
work. As he does so, he finds that 'two words leap out of the
text of the preface as evident markers of Luke's intention:
the words "fulfilled" and "certainty".' The subject of the
work is those things which 'have been fulfilled among us'; its
aim is to allow Theophilus and others like him to perceive
the certainty, the reliability, of the message they have
heard.[11]

In the same way, the first episode in Luke's second
volume, viz. Acts 1.1–11, can be seen to have an altogether
new force when it is read in the light of the purposes which
appear to have governed his overall work. We have already
spoken in Chapter 2 of Luke's manifest concern in Acts to
emphasize the God-given origin of the Gentile mission, and
while noting that different scholars differ in their understanding of the precise circle of readers whom Luke was

seeking to convince of this truth, have opted for the view that he is addressing Christians who are looking wistfully over their shoulders and wondering ruefully whether the Gentile mission, which has led to the final separation between church and synagogue, has not been a great mistake.[12]

But, however we envisage Luke's primary readership, the first episode of Acts, which tells of Jesus's commissioning of the disciples and his ascension, acquires an altogether new force and point, once we recognize the desire to vindicate the Gentile mission as a dominant concern of Luke's total enterprise. Note how clearly it sets forth the divine origin of the mission. The outreach of the Christian community to the ends of the earth is not due to the quirks of some of its founding members who had quixotic ideas. It represents the obedient response of the church to the commission of its heavenly Lord. The way which the church has actually followed is no wrong turning, it is the way which the Lord himself prescribed for it. There has been no mistake.

This episode acquires a still sharper point in the light of other dimensions of the overall purpose Luke appears to have been pursuing. While the evidence may not be sufficient to allow us to say that Luke is dealing with a crisis caused by the delay of the parousia, there is still good reason to believe that the readers he has chiefly in mind were uncertain what to believe about the present status of Christ and the ongoing purpose of God. Where is Jesus and what is he doing? What time is this in which we are living and what are we to hope for?[13]

To any readers of Acts who were troubled by such questions this opening episode must have brought powerful reassurance. As for Jesus, though withdrawn from our sight, he is no absentee Lord but seated at the right hand of the Father and engaged in powerful intercourse with his people in the world, carrying on what he began to do and teach in the days of his flesh through the Spirit, who is his representative, and the church, which is his instrument. And therefore this time in which we are living is not a hiatus, a gap during which God is holding his breath, so to speak, but a time in which the church must be about its God-given commission to carry the good news of salvation to the ends of the earth.

As a further example of how a passage acquires new depth of meaning when read in the light of the total work of which it is part, I cite Heb. 13.8: 'Jesus Christ is the same yesterday and today and for ever.' The link between this verse and the immediate context is clear. In the previous verse the author calls upon his (or her) readers to remember those who had been their leaders in earlier times but were now dead. Deprived of their immediate example, their teaching and their support, those who remained clearly had a painful sense of emptiness, and of apprehension, as they looked to the future. Who was to guide them from now on? And so this author, who has just urged them to keep fresh the memory of their leaders, now reminds them that if men and women depart Christ remains. Yesterday he was the inspiration and strength of their leaders who are now dead. He is that still for each of the readers of the letter. He will be that, as effectively, tomorrow and always. Others serve their generation by the will of God and pass on; he remains, the same yesterday and today and for ever.

But there is also a link between this verse and the argument of the letter as a whole. This letter lays a remarkable stress not only on what Jesus Christ has meant, has been, for those who believe in him but also on what he is and will continue to be. Again and again, as he speaks of Jesus, the author uses the perfect tense, the form of the verb which stresses the ongoing results of a past action (1.4; 2.9, 18; 4.14, 15; 7.26, 28; 9.26; 12.2). Two words express his purpose in a nutshell, the words, 'Consider Jesus' (3.1; 12.2f.). That is just what he is doing throughout the letter, inviting his readers to consider Jesus as a figure not only of the past but of the present and the future too. Consider him who is God's final word to mankind (1.1–4).

Consider him who is not ashamed to own us as his brothers and sisters (2.10–13).

Consider him who has not only taken our side but who now sits at God's side, where he for ever pleads our cause (4.14–16; 7.23–25).

Consider him who is the same yesterday and today and for ever. This is the theme to which the author keeps returning, the thought of what Jesus Christ has been for his people and is and will continue to be, of what he has done for them and is doing and will continue to do. Therefore the declaration of 13.8 sums up in a remarkable way the thrust of the letter as a whole.

If we see that, we will be in less danger of misinterpreting its key-word, the word 'same'. For there is sameness and sameness. A frozen pond stays the same; so does a dead sheep. That is one kind of sameness, the sameness of immobility, of death. But there is also another kind of sameness, the sameness of constancy, of consistency, of reliability – the sameness of life. When this author writes that Jesus Christ is the same, just as when other authors in the Bible declare that God is unchanging, he (or she) – and they – do not mean that he is frozen into immobility, still less that he is dead. They mean rather that he is unchanging in his faithfulness. Amid all the changes of history he remains faithful. He keeps his promises.

The Risk of Oversimplifying

In the foregoing discussion we have described the goal of exegesis as being to attain an understanding of a passage as a whole or of the intention underlying the whole, while emphasizing at the same time that one can only hope to reach such an understanding through testing one's intuitions about the author's intention against what he has said and left unsaid. But the question may still be asked whether it is ever possible to formulate a concept of a passage as a whole or of the intention underlying it without some distortion, especially if, as we have just maintained, the hermeneutical process is a never-ending one. Some passages in Paul's letters, in particular, are extraordinarily complex and represent anything but a straightforward, linear development. Consider, for example, the variety of emotions Paul expresses in II Cor. 5.1–10: expectation of new life beyond death (v.1); weariness with earthly existence (v.2); shrinking from the possibility of death (vv.3f.); confidence that God will fulfil his purpose for us (v.5); longing to be with the Lord, mingled with a confidence which nothing can shake (vv.6–8); ambition to be well-pleasing to him, before whose judgment seat we must all one day stand (vv.9–10). Yet in the end all these conflicting emotions seem to recede before one overriding desire, viz. the desire, whatever may be his circumstances, to be well-pleasing to the Lord.

Allo writes of this passage that Paul is haunted from the beginning by the thought of the judgment of God,[14] but Didier seems to catch the dominant mood of the passage better when he writes that the accent is on how we ought to abandon ourselves to the hands of the Father, who knows better than we do what is good for us. Whatever the fears and desires which arise in his heart, the Christian will have complete confidence in him who gives him the earnest of the Spirit and takes charge of his destiny.[15]

Capturing the Mood

It is indeed essential to capture the dominant mood and direction of a passage like this, if one is not to misconstrue the individual verses of which it is composed. For example, I can recall hearing a sermon on Rom. 10.9 which placed all the emphasis on the words 'mouth' and 'heart', thus: to be a true Christian you must not be a silent witness but make open confession with your words; your belief in the resurrection must be not merely a matter of the head but of the heart. Such an interpretation of verse 9, however, runs clean counter to the dominant direction of the whole paragraph of which it is part.

The dominant thought of the paragraph running from verse 5 to verse 13 is a contrast between two ways of attaining righteousness, the way of law and the way of faith. The first way promises righteousness to the doer of the law, the second asks no more than a genuine acceptance of the gospel. Paul finds both of these ways articulated in the Old Testament, viz. in Lev. 18.5 and Deut. 30.1–12, with a further echo in Deut. 9.4. His interpretation of the passage from Deuteronomy 30 is particularly striking. The main thrust of that passage is that the law of God is not remote or inaccessible but near, known and therefore practicable. Paul reinterprets the words of Deuteronomy first in terms of Christ (vv.6f.), then in terms of the gospel (v.8). The point of verses 6f. is that it is Christ who is not remote, either in heaven or in the realm of the dead.

We know of rabbis who taught that if all Israel were to keep the law perfectly for one day the Messiah would come. But the whole of the preceding argument of Romans has shown that God did not wait for a perfect fulfilment of the law before he sent his son but sent him to live and die for men and women while they were still weak, still sinners, still ungodly (5.6–8). Through the glorious deed of the Father and the Father alone Christ has been raised from the dead (6.4).

How then is one to find righteousness, salvation, through him? Reinterpreting Deuteronomy 30 once more but remaining faithful to the essential emphasis of the passage, Paul declares, 'The word is near, on your lips and on your heart, that is the word of faith which we proclaim' (v.8). God did not require humanity to scale Everests of obedience before he sent his Son. Nor does he ask heroic feats of those who, in response to the gospel, look to him for salvation. All he asks is the confessing mouth and the believing heart.

The dominant thought of the whole paragraph to which this verse belongs is not that of how much one needs to do to be a Christian but how little.

Polarities

As early as in the second chapter we were led to define the art of exegesis in terms of holding different concerns in a fruitful tension: the concern for intention and the concern for the text; the concern for this passage and the concern for the total biblical witness. In the same way, in our discussion of literary form in Chapter 3, we spoke of the need to develop a feel for this writing both in its similarity to other writings and in its distinctiveness. The theme of the present chapter has been the possibility of fruitful interaction between attention to the whole and attention to the parts. The notion of holding different concerns in fruitful tension will also dominate the next chapter, in which we will speak of the past and the present.

5

Past and Present

The Use and Value of Tradition

I have had occasion more than once to speak of some of the writings of the New Testament being the product of a lengthy historical process. This is most obviously true of the Synoptic Gospels, as we saw in our discussions of form criticism and redaction criticism in Chapter 2, but there is reason to think that Paul too has incorporated a number of items of early Christian tradition into his letters – confessional traditions, baptismal traditions and hymns, as well as lists of virtues and vices and exhortations. It appears to have been a particular concern of his, especially in Romans, to demonstrate his fundamental agreement with earlier utterances of faith and thereby to remind his hearers and readers of the common foundations of faith.

Whenever there is reason to suspect the presence of earlier traditions, whether in the Synoptics or the letters of Paul or wherever, the question inevitably arises, 'What weight should be given to them in exegesis?' What I have written so far has been based on the assumption that the primary focus of the exegete should be on the final form of the text, that is, on the author of the work in question and on what he has made of the materials he had to work with rather than on those materials themselves. Such a view commends itself the more strongly, the more the evangelists are seen, as they now are by almost all scholars, as writers with pronounced literary skills, theological perspectives and pastoral concerns. It should be noted that Paul too, while incorporating earlier traditions into his letters, has by no means taken them over uncritically but has provided them with interpretative additions, so that a clear distinction needs to be drawn between the theology implicit in the tradition and the theological standpoint of Paul himself.

Witnesses in their own Right

I do not wish to suggest, however, that the only function of the earlier traditions is to help us to discern more clearly the distinctive emphases of the later writers. It is clear that they do serve such a purpose, and it is an important one. For example, many scholars hold that, in view of its content and vocabulary, Rom. 3.25 (some would say vv.24 and 25 and perhaps the beginning of v.26 as well) should be regarded as a piece of earlier tradition which Paul has incorporated into his argument. All scholars who hold any form of this theory are agreed that the phrase *dia pisteōs*, which dislocates the flow of words, has been inserted by Paul himself. If Paul did make this insertion, then that is further evidence of the weight he attached to faith as the only way to appropriate the saving event. Yet the tradition which Paul has here incorporated, if indeed he has done so, should surely be regarded as having more than the function of a piece of litmus paper, which brings into clearer view the distinctive theology of the apostle; it too should be regarded as a witness in its own right. From the very fact that it was preserved in a recognizable form we can fairly conclude that it was heard as the word of God by the community of faith which used it.

For the Christian readers of the Gospels the earliest level of the tradition is of particular interest and importance, for it is this level that brings us closest to the words and works of Jesus himself. If Jesus is indeed the word of God incarnate, the critical Christian reader will not be content merely to hear Jesus as presented to us by Matthew or Mark or Luke or John. He or she will want to get as close as possible to the historical situation in which Jesus lived, in order to hear how he spoke to that situation and how he would have been heard in it.

In dealing with the teaching contained in the Gospels it is often possible to distinguish three layers of meaning: the meaning intended by Jesus himself in the setting of his historical ministry, the meaning intended by early Christian teachers and preachers in the context of the mission of the early church and the meaning intended by the evangelist himself in the context of his Gospel. In distinguishing these various layers, modern critical scholarship has multiplied the range of options open to the preacher, providing more options than most preachers care to take advantage of.[1] The Jesus level of the tradition ought to be of peculiar interest and importance not only to the theologian but the preacher too. For many students of theology Jeremias's book on the parables remains not only the most exciting book he ever wrote but one of the most exciting theological books they have ever read, precisely because of the hope it offers of uncovering in parable after parable, the original intention of Jesus, which has been obscured by overlays of later interpretation. The enthusiastic commendation of the publishers, comparing Jeremias to the restorer of an old masterpiece, which I quoted somewhat critically in Chapter 3,[2] does reflect faithfully the excitement generated among the first readers of the book in the fifties.

The Primacy of the Final Form

With these qualifications made, however, we return to our main point that even in the Gospels and still more in the epistles the primary focus of the exegete should be on the author himself and what he has made of the materials at his disposal rather than on the materials themselves. There are both theological and practical reasons for such a concentration. The fact that it is the finished work which has been preserved rather than the earlier traditions which have gone into its composition is surely of theological importance. Furthermore, in dealing with the finished work we are on firm ground, whereas any attempt to identify an earlier level is bound to be to some extent speculative.

Plethora of Hypotheses

This is a point which is worth stressing, since there are some passages in the New Testament which have generated so many hypotheses about underlying *'Vorlagen'*, i.e. earlier traditional formulations, that it is very easy to get lost in the details of conflicting theories. One such passage has already been mentioned, Rom. 3.24–26. In 1972 John Ziesler observed that the theory that in these verses Paul is glossing an earlier formulation 'is somewhat endangered by the multiplication of hypotheses',[3] and since then a number of further variations of the theory have been proposed. The *Festschrift* in honour of Ernst Käsemann alone contains two.[4]

Words with a Past

I have spoken of passages in the New Testament which appear to be the product of a long process of composition. But what about the basic units of the language of the New Testament, the words themselves? They too have a history. Any writer in the Greek language in the first century AD was heir to a written literary tradition centuries old, as well as an oral literary tradition reaching back still further into the past. For Jews and Christians the whole of the Old Testament was available in Greek versions, and the very process of translation had, as we shall see, enriched still further the meaning of a number of Greek words. The whole of this vocabulary, in all its richness and diversity, stood at the disposal of the writers of the New Testament. To perceive the full significance of this linguistic history for exegesis, however, we need to be clear about some basic semantic principles.

Multiple Meanings

Something which is fundamental to semantics (i.e. the systematic study of the meaning of words) is the recognition that, as Ronald Knox has put it, 'every common word in every living language has not one meaning but a quantity of shades of meaning'.[5] The French writer, de Saussure, in reaction against what he considered an excessively diachronic approach to the meaning of a text, that is, an approach to its meaning through history, the history of its author, the history of its composition, the history of its component parts, has used the analogy of a game of chess. To understand the situation at any stage of a game of chess, he argues, all you need to know is the present location of the pieces on the board. Any information about how the various pieces came to be in their present position is completely irrelevant.[6] While recognizing some force in his overall argument, we must surely say that any image which suggests an analogy between words and chessmen can be singularly misleading. For the value of a chessman to a player can be strictly and exhaustively defined. Any knight may move in this direction but not that, any pawn in this direction but not that. And all this remains true of all chessmen anywhere, whatever the material of which they are made, whether it be wood or ivory or porcelain. But words are not like that. Their value, their meaning, cannot be strictly and exhaustively defined once and for all. To quote Ronald Knox once again,

> Words are not coins, dead things whose value can be mathematically computed. You cannot quote an exact English equivalent for a French word, as you might quote an exact English equivalent for a French coin. Words are living things, full of shades of meaning, full of associations, and, what is more, they are apt to change their significance from one generation to the next.[7]

Not One-to-One

What is of especial importance to any translator or anyone reading a translated text is the further principle that the range of meanings conveyed by a word in one language rarely coincides with the range of meanings conveyed by its nearest equivalent in another. Hence this word in the original language will not be invariably translated by that word in the receptor language but by several words, possibly quite a number. The Greek verb *katargeō*, which is not of particularly frequent occurrence, being found in the New Testament only twenty-seven times in all, and which means, as a first approximation, to make ineffective, powerless, idle, is translated in the Authorized Version in no fewer than seventeen different ways.[8] The Greek word *logos*, which

occurs three hundred and thirty-one times, is translated in
the Authorized Version in no fewer than twenty-two ways.[9]
We can therefore appreciate the sentiments expressed by
Ronald Knox in the sentences immediately following those
which I have just quoted.

> The translator who understands his job feels constantly
> like Alice in Wonderland trying to play croquet with
> flamingoes for mallets and hedgehogs for balls. Words are
> for ever eluding his grasp.[10]

A Matter of Convention

The reason why a word in one language rarely covers exactly
the same range of meanings as its nearest equivalent in
another is that, with the partial exception of onomatopoeic
words, the relationship between the forms of a language and
the meanings which they express is one of convention, of use
and wont. This is a third basic principle of semantics. There
is, in other words, no logic inherent in the nature of language
which makes it inevitable that this word 'table' should refer
to this object with a flat top and four legs. The only reason
why it does convey such a meaning is that the speakers of the
English language do in fact use the word to refer to such an
object.

The conventional nature of the relationship between the
forms of a language and the meanings which they express
becomes clearer when we recall that the same word can
convey different meanings in different English-speaking
countries. A 'port' in Australia may mean a harbour or it may
mean a trunk; a 'trunk' in America may mean a part of a car
or a part of an elephant. Furthermore, the meaning of a word
can change quite markedly in the course of centuries. More
often than not, the range of meanings which a word conveys
expands. Sometimes it contracts. The meaning of the word
'conversation' has clearly contracted since the seventeenth
century, when it commended itself to the King James
translators as a rendering of the Greek word *politeuma* in
Phil. 3.20, which suggests, among other things, corporate
being, association. Of these three semantic principles it is

the first and the second which are most directly relevant to the task of exegesis. Every common word in Greek or Hebrew has not one meaning but a quantity of shades of meaning, which can rarely, if ever, be conveyed by a single English equivalent. This principle must be kept constantly in mind, especially when we are dealing with any word of theological significance, if our understanding of it is not to be seriously impoverished. Furthermore, to appreciate the richness and depth of meaning capable of being conveyed by a word of theological significance in any passage we are studying, we need to expose ourselves as fully as we can to the range of meanings which it conveys in earlier writings.

A Double Shift

The situation is complicated by the fact that we are dealing with three languages: Hebrew, Greek and English. We may not assume, as a matter of course, that the full range of meanings capable of being conveyed by this Hebrew word *a* was apparent to the makers of the LXX (or other) translations when they chose to render it by the Greek words *b* and *c*; or, even if it was, that the Greek words were thereby permanently invested with a richer range of potential meanings.[11] Again and again, however, we find Greek words being used first in the LXX and then later in the New Testament to convey meanings for which the usage of those words in secular Greek affords no real parallel.

Justify

Take, for example, the Greek word *dikaioun*, usually translated as 'justify'. A quick glance at passages like Rom. 2.12f.; 3.19f.; 8.33f.; I Cor. 4.3–5, where there is a contrast, explicit or implicit, between being justified and being found guilty before God, suggests that Paul is using the word to mean something like 'declare righteous'. To that use of the word there is no exact parallel in secular Greek usage. In secular Greek the verb *dikaioun* carries two main meanings: first, (with an impersonal object) to hold right and reasonable, to deem or pronounce right, to decide to do, to claim as a right;[12] secondly, (with a personal object) to treat justly, nearly always with the negative sense, to condemn.[13] The first of these uses affords a partial parallel to Paul, but the second amounts to the direct opposite. Clearly Paul's use of the word *dikaioun* has been largely determined by some other factor than the use of *dikaioun* in secular Greek. That other factor is undoubtedly the regular use of *dikaioun* in the LXX to translate either the Hiph'il or the Pi'el form of *tsádaq*, both of which most commonly denote the action of a judge in pronouncing in favour of one of the parties to a legal dispute.

Glory

Another word which acquired a significant extension of meaning through being used in the LXX to translate a Hebrew word is the word *doxa*. In classical Greek the word means essentially opinion or reputation, but in the LXX it is used to render the Hebrew word *kábód*, which, from Ezekiel on, denotes particularly the splendour of the divine presence. Not only is this use carried on into the New Testament, there is, as Caird shows, some evidence that this development in the meaning of the word affected even the vernacular Greek of the pagan environment. Some magical texts from Egypt use the word in the sense of radiance or splendour.[14]

Problems of Translation

Our main problem, however, as exegetes and preachers, is how to plumb and then express in English words the depth and richness of meaning which the Greek and Hebrew words are capable of conveying, always alert to the possibility, indeed the probability, that they will have a peculiar force and emphasis which no single English word is adequate to express. Let a few examples suffice to illustrate the point.

We have already suggested that Paul uses the word *dikaioun* to mean something like 'declare righteous'. While that rendering is not wrong, it falls far short of expressing the strong positive connotations which the Greek word has acquired in the Bible from its Hebrew antecedents. The prophets of Israel are constantly protesting against the perversion of justice, against malicious accusation, and against judges who take bribes, who refuse the poor their rights and who turn judgment to wormwood.[15] Accordingly, the righteous judge was honoured not so much because he had shown a truly judicial impartiality but because he had rescued an innocent person from oppression, delivering the needy when he cried and the humble when he had no helper. By pronouncing in favour of the innocent party, he took his side against those who were trying to destroy him. The simple declaration, 'You are in the right', the declaration denoted by the verb *hitsdiq*, 'justify', was seen as a signal act of succour. In Paul's letters too the word carries strong positive connotations. Note how in Rom. 8.31, 33 the words, 'It is God who justifies', have as their counterpart in the parallelism the words 'It is God who is on our side'. Equally strongly positive are the connotations attaching to the word 'righteousness', the word used to describe the conduct of anyone who does right by another and therefore of the judge who judges rightly, but more particularly, especially in Second Isaiah and the Psalms, of the God of Israel, who stands by his covenant people. How strong these connotations are is strikingly demonstrated by Psalm 69.27, in which the psalmist prays that the wicked may not enter into Yahweh's righteousness. If the word 'righteousness' had conveyed for him any suggestion of punishment, that is precisely what he would have craved for the wicked. Anyone who tried to understand Paul's message of the righteousness of God without taking this history of word use into account would be seriously impoverished in his understanding, especially since there is reason to think that in Rom. 1.16–17 Paul is adapting the language of Psalm 98.[16]

The same sort of thing can also be said about the word 'glory'. To most readers, the phrase 'the glory of God' probably suggests God's otherness, God's unapproachability, that which makes him Creator not creature. That is certainly an ingredient of the meaning of the expression as used in the older parts of the Old Testament, for example, Deut. 5.24. What is not apparent to the uninstructed reader is that, largely through the influence of Ezekiel, the word comes to be closely associated with the idea of revelation. Thereafter the word is used again and again to denote that which makes the invisible God visible, that which reveals him or makes him known, whether it be a natural phenomenon (Ps. 29.1–3) or a place, like the temple (I Kings 8.10f.; Ps. 24.7–10) or an event, like the exodus (Ex. 24.15–18) or the deliverance from exile (Isa. 40.5) or some event yet to occur (Isa. 59.19; 60.1–5; Ezek. 43.1–5).[17] Once again, to read a passage like John 1.11, which speaks of the glory of the word made flesh, without taking into account this history of word use is to be impoverished in one's understanding.

I have been stressing the importance of exposing oneself as fully as possible to the range of meanings conveyed by the Hebrew counterparts to the Greek words used in the New Testament, at least those of theological significance, in order to appreciate the richness and depth of meaning which they are capable of conveying. As in the first section of this chapter, however, so here too this emphasis on the past must be held in tension with an emphasis on the present. Our aim remains that of determining as precisely as possible what this word means in this passage, and that question cannot be settled by an exploration of its use in earlier literature and of the Hebrew words which it translates in the LXX. Such an exploration, as we have already implied, can do no more than indicate the meanings it is capable of conveying.

Nor should it be assumed that all the shades of meaning conveyed by a word in earlier literature are present in the intention of a biblical writer when he uses a word in any particular context. This was one of the common fallacies in biblical exegesis identified by James Barr in his important book *The Semantics of Biblical Language*. He calls it the fallacy of the unitary concept. Closely allied to it is what he calls the root fallacy, viz. the assumption that the root of a word is necessarily determinative of its meaning throughout its history. He has little difficulty in showing that words often move out of any recognizable contact with their origins.[18]

If, then, the history of a word's use cannot be taken as determining the question of its meaning in this passage, where are we to turn? A knowledge of the way in which this author uses this word in other passages is certainly important. Even more important are the semantic clues provided by the actual context, such as the presence of words which appear to be synonymous with the word in question or are contrasted with it. For example, as we have already noted, there are several places in Paul's letters where the word 'justify' or a word cognate with it is contrasted with the idea of condemnation. This contrast is an important clue to the meaning of the words in question in the context (see Rom. 2.12f.; 3.19f.; 8.33f.; I Cor. 4.3–5; II Cor. 3.9).

At the same time one should always be alert to the possibility that a word is being used to convey a nuance to which earlier usage affords no exact parallel, always open (to use Gadamer's phrase) to 'the experience of being pulled up short by the text', which is a sign that a word is being used in a way to which we are not accustomed.[19]

Words and Concepts

As with words, so also with concepts. Attention to the past, to the history of the concept in question, needs to be held in tension with attention to the present, to the precise way in which the concept is being presented in this particular passage. But first a word about the distinction between concepts and words.

One of the many services which James Barr rendered to biblical scholars by his book, *The Semantics of Biblical Language*, was to underline the importance of this distinction. He shows clearly that to penetrate to the heart of the thought of a biblical writer it is not sufficient to study the history and use of the particular words which make up his vocabulary. 'It is the sentence', he writes, '(and of course the still larger literary complex, such as the complete speech or poem) which is the linguistic bearer of the usual theological statement, and not the word.'[20] The uniqueness of Christian preaching is not to be found primarily in the new words which it issued nor in the new meanings which it imparted to old words but rather in the new ways in which it combined old words. In these new combinations the meaning of the component words often changed only slightly or not at all, the new or distinctive concept being indicated by the word – combination.

To illustrate the point once again by a word from the righteousness family, in Rom. 4.5 Paul refers to God as justifying the ungodly. This expression is clearly borrowed from the Old Testament (see Ex. 23.7; Isa. 5.23). In the Old Testament passages which Paul is echoing, the word 'justify' has a clearly forensic meaning, referring to the verdict of a judge. There is no reason to suppose that Paul intends the word to have anything other than a forensic meaning either. Nevertheless, the expression as a whole is being used to convey a startling, new concept of God and his ways with sinners. In Ex. 23.7 and Isa. 5.23 it refers to the practice of unjust judges, in Paul it is a description of God. It is not that the individual words which Paul uses have been invested with a new meaning but rather that they have been inserted into a quite different context and used to convey a quite different concept.

This distinction between words and concepts is one which needs to be kept constantly in mind. We need to ask of every passage we are reading not only 'What theologically significant words does it contain?' but 'What concepts are central to it? What are the theological issues with which it is wrestling? Are there any other issues, not central to the author's purpose, on which it also throws light?' It may well be that the actual words the author uses will themselves provide us with an answer to that question, but they may not. We must always look at the passage as a whole and ask, 'What is it all about?' One of the central biblical concepts is that of election. With increasing clarity one can trace the emergence, especially in Second Isaiah and Jonah, of the conviction that God has chosen Israel as an act of grace, for purpose as well as privilege and for the sake of the salvation of the world. This concept is largely conveyed by the word *báchar*, the subject of an important study by the Dutch scholar, Vriezen.[21] However, the same concept of the responsibilities entailed by Yahweh's gracious election of Israel also finds expression in a verse in Amos which makes no use of *báchar*, viz Amos 3.2: 'You only have I known of all the families of the earth; therefore I will punish you for all your iniquities.'

The Shock of the New

As with words, so also with concepts it is when an awareness of the past is combined with an alertness to the actuality of this text that the perception of the new becomes possible. The more I know about the history of a concept, the more clearly I will perceive what is distinctive about the understanding of it which is implicit in the passage I am studying. This emphasis, which we have made in each of the major sections of this chapter, on the possibility of fruitful interaction between attention to the old and attention to the new can be seen to be still more important in the light of Stephen Prickett's remarkable book, *Words and the Word*.

In the preface to the *Good News Bible* the reader is assured that 'every effort has been made to use language that is natural, clear, simple and unambiguous'.[22] It is Prickett's contention that the Bible is precisely not about things that are 'natural, clear, simple and unambiguous' but about events so baffling as to imply quite new ways of seeing the world.[23] According to the testimony of the Bible, the experience of God is an experience of 'disconfirmation'.[24] That is to say, 'it involves the discovery or disclosure that a whole way of seeing and feeling to which one is personally committed is undermined or made to appear partial, inadequate or irrelevant'.[25] 'The experience of disconfirmation is a paradigm biblical event'.[26]

The story of Elijah at Horeb is cited as emblematic of such events, which occur throughout the Bible.[27] Elijah's original assumptions are disconfirmed by a revelation so ambiguous as to resist any modern attempt to reduce it to a direct, simple statement. He has come from Carmel, where God has answered by fire, but here God is not in the fire, nor the wind nor the earthquake. Yet from whom, if not from him, did these things come? His presence, when it is at last revealed, is experienced as 'something mysteriously apart from the world of natural phenomena',[28] yet not as something wholly visionary or supernatural. The revelation resists classification in terms of our modern categories – either a miracle or a vision, either natural or supernatural. What Elijah hears is best rendered as 'a voice of thin silence'.[29] Prickett finds echoes of this story, and equally striking examples of disconfirmation, in certain passages from European literature, particularly in Dante's account of his meeting with Beatrice on the threshold of Paradise. There Dante experiences a shattering disconfirmation of all his expectations and self respect. 'Dante is stressing here', Prickett writes, 'the sheer disconcertingness of revelation. The natural reason of man is utterly confounded by the overpowering "otherness" of the transcendent.'[30]

To describe the disconcertingness of revelation Prickett also borrows from Berggren the term 'stereoscopy' or 'stereoscopic vision', that is, 'the ability to entertain two different points of view at the same time'.[31] As an example of stereoscopy Prickett cites another incident from Dante, in which the poet sees a griffin one way with his own eyes and another way with the eyes of Beatrice.[32] Prickett reads both the account of Dante's meeting with Beatrice and the vision of the two-fold griffin as 'a metaphor of a certain kind of religious experience where the same event must be seen in two very different ways at the same time if either is to be understood at all'.[33] Such experiences can only be described in the language of disconfirmation, stereoscopy, ambiguity. Moreover, they can only be apprehended afresh by someone who is alert to such language, that is to 'the new formulation, the fresh phrase, the startling conjunction'.[34] Only through being alert to such things can we begin to experience for ourselves the impact of the original event, the 'shock of the new'. The translator, above all, must be alert to the new, to 'those cases where there is no equivalent, because what is being said is strange and without parallel, struggling to painful birth in the original language'.[35] The alert reader of the Bible will certainly be pulled up short again and again by what Prickett calls the language of disconfirmation or stereoscopy. Consider, for example, Paul's words in Phil. 2.12bf.: 'work out your own salvation with fear and trembling; for God is at work in you, both to will and to work for his good pleasure.' Is our salvation our business or is it God's business? In one breath Paul speaks as if it were our business and ours alone, in the next as if it were God's and his alone. To heighten the paradox he links the two clauses not with 'although', which might suggest a co-operation between ourselves and God, but with 'for': make your salvation your business for God has made it his.

Nevertheless, the struggle to give full weight to each clause at the same time does yield insight. Read by itself, the first clause would amount to a call to salvation through one's own efforts, and the words 'fear and trembling' would denote fear of failure and rejection. But the meaning of this clause is profoundly changed when it is read in conjunction with the second. The exhortation to work out your own salvation now means something like, 'Let God have his way, put no obstacles in his path', while the words 'fear and trembling' now denote not the fear of failure and rejection but the awe of the person who finds that he or she is standing on holy ground, the shaken humility of one in whom God has begun his transforming work. Thus the startling conjunctions of this passage bear eloquent witness to 'the sheer disconcertingness of revelation'. The attentive reader will be constantly on the alert for such signs of the impact of the transcendent on the language of the Bible.

The Shock of the New and the Canon

Disconfirmation, stereoscopy, the new formulation, the fresh phrase, the startling conjunction – it is these qualities, above all, which I miss when I turn from the New Testament to the post-biblical writings.

Let Phil. 2.12b serve once more as an example. Paradoxically, Paul holds together here the sovereignty of grace and the need for human response, but, as the history of Christian thought in the following centuries shows, it is all too easy to destroy this tension by emphasizing one side at the expense of the other. On the one hand, faith can be turned into a Christian virtue. The believer then merits salvation on the ground of his faith. It is equally possible, from anxiety to exclude the idea of merit, to exclude all initiative whatsoever on the human side and, in T. W. Manson's words, 'treat man as a mere bottle to be filled with the water of life'.[36] If Augustine at times errs in the latter direction, most of the post-biblical writers err in the former. Thus for Barnabas it is presumptuous for Christians to think of themselves as justified already; justification is a future affair, and they have to prove themselves worthy.[37] Even Origen, who at times seems to have considerable insight into the meaning of faith, teaches that pardon is for those who are worthy or have made themselves worthy to receive it. He lists seven means through which Christians can secure pardon: baptism, martyrdom, alms-giving, the mutual forgiveness of believers, the forgiveness that follows amendment, much love, and, lastly, penitence and confession.[38] In the light of such statements the aphorism of Campbell Moody (itself based on Harnack) seems fully justified: 'The contrast between Law and Faith was understood by none but Marcion; and by him it was misunderstood.'[39]

All this is highly relevant to preaching, to which we are about to turn, and in particular, to the question whether preaching ought to be uniquely dependent on the biblical witness. In this respect, as well as others, I believe that the canon imposes itself. This is not to say that the Bible would not have played the part which it has played in the life of the church if it had included some writings which it does not now include or had excluded some which it now contains. What I do believe is that what lies centrally and solidly within the boundaries of the Bible has a unique and irreplaceable importance for the church's continuing task of proclamation.

Our discussion of exegesis is now completed. In Chapter 2 we considered the aims of exegesis. In the last three chapters we have been considering in turn three important aspects of the practice of exegesis. In all four chapters we have spoken of the need to hold different emphases in fruitful tension: intention and text, the typical and the particular, whole and parts, past and present. In the concluding two chapters we shall turn our attention to preaching and to the ways in which one can move responsibly to preaching from exegesis.

6

Why Preach?

Obsolete?

There have been many signs over the last two or three
decades of a crisis of confusion about the place of preaching
in the life of our churches. In 1979, for example, a discussion
about preaching ran on for months in *Church and Nation*,
the journal of the Victorian Synod of the Uniting Church in
Australia, sparked off by an article by Ben Draper entitled
'The Pulpit in Eclipse'. 'Preaching', he wrote, 'or the feeble-
ness, dullness, misguidedness, barrenness and in some cases
the plain absence of it, is at least intimately linked with
many of the ills in the church in our time.'

In the pulpit, uncertainty about the use of preaching; in the
pew, dissatisfaction with the preacher's performance – we
should not imagine that these things are peculiar to our own
country. It would not be difficult to assemble a number of
trenchant expressions of these sentiments from the recent
theological literature of a church which has always given to
the preaching of the word the highest place, viz. the
Evangelical Church in Germany. In 1959 Gerhard Ebeling
wrote these words:

> We need only consider our own experiences quite coolly in
> order to conclude that we have to bring a certain measure
> of goodwill to the average sermon, if we are not to be bored
> or furious, sarcastic or melancholy in our reactions. What
> an expenditure of effort is put into the preaching of the
> Christian faith up and down the land! But – again with

exceptions – is it not the institutionally assured platitudes which are preached?[1]

A decade later another German writer imagines a preacher offering his congregation the following 'sermon':

Liebe Gemeinde (my dear brothers and sisters), every Sunday you hear 'bla – bla – bla'. I too hear 'bla   bla   bla', because what I have to say is 'bla – bla – bla'. This Sunday let us for once be silent.[2]

Such expressions of frustration need to be heard with the utmost seriousness. We dare not assume that the place of preaching in the life of our churches is assured, so that the only question that need concern us is, 'How should we go about it?'

As a first step, however, it is essential for us to be clear about what we are talking about. Many a discussion about preaching in which I have taken part has proved inconclusive because the participants have meant different things by preaching and thus found themselves talking at cross purposes. Moreover, some of the criticisms commonly levelled at preaching reveal, in my judgment, that the critic is labouring under an inadequate conception of what preaching is about and therefore expecting the wrong things from it.

Towards a Definition of Preaching

But what is preaching? That question cannot be settled by a simple appeal to the Bible. The fact is that preaching has evolved over the centuries and only by degrees attained a clearly defined form. That form results from the confluence over some generations of several lines of tradition: the process of translating and explaining the scriptures initiated by Ezra and carried on in synagogue sermons (cf. Neh. 8.7–8); the ministries of missionary proclamation, teaching and prophecy (all central to the life of the early church but with roots in the life of ancient Israel); and ancient Greek rhetoric.[3] This means that, as normally practised today, preaching does not correspond exactly to any one of the various ministries of the word about which we read in the

New Testament but has elements of them all. However, some features of those ministries are sufficiently striking to deserve to be given considerable weight in shaping our understanding of preaching.

The principal forms of ministry of the word referred to in the New Testament appear to be those denoted by the words *kērygma* (missionary proclamation), *didachē* (teaching) and *prophēteia* (prophecy). The first term denotes, in Dodd's words, 'the public proclamation of Christianity to the non-Christian world'.[4] The sermons preached by Peter and Paul in Acts are examples of *kērygma*. Teaching was defined by Dodd largely in terms of ethics, but it is generally agreed nowadays that that definition is too narrow. The main difference between missionary proclamation and teaching, as practised in New Testament times, appears to lie not so much in the content of what is proclaimed or taught as in the audience at which it is directed. 'Teaching' normally denotes an activity addressed to believers and appears to have included not only the content of the *kērygma* but all those matters in which the community needed to be instructed. Hebrews 6.2 implies that these included not only ethical instruction but teaching concerning the sacraments and the last things.[5] The Sermon on the Mount is an example of Christian teaching, but the complete Gospels, insofar as they appear to be addressed primarily to believers, can also be so classified. The prophet on the other hand declares to this community the message which he believes the risen Christ would say to them at this moment. The letters to the seven churches in chapters 2 and 3 of Revelation are examples of Christian prophecy.

A Word that is Concrete

None of these various forms of ministry of the word consists of the repetition of the same message over and over again in the same words. On the contrary, the message is adapted to the particular situation of the hearers.

It is clear from Paul's letters that the missionary proclamation addressed to Gentile Christians took a different form from that addressed to Jewish Christians. In the first four chapters of both Romans and I Corinthians Paul draws the same fundamental contrast, viz., between reliance on oneself and reliance on God, between trusting in one's own achievements and trusting in the achievements of God, but the terms in which he sets forth this contrast are strikingly different. In Romans he speaks of righteousness and justification and law, of faith and works, in I Corinthians of wisdom and folly. But though the terminology is different, the aim is the same: to demolish a false self-reliance. Whereas Romans attacks boasting of one's works (Rom. 3.19), I Corinthians attacks boasting of one's wisdom (I Cor. 1.29,31). In the one epistle the cross is the condemnation of the righteousness of mankind, in the other the condemnation of the wisdom of the world. Whereas in Romans it is through the renunciation of righteousness that one attains righteousness, in I Corinthians it is through the surrender of one's own wisdom that one receives wisdom (I Cor. 3.18). The one epistle offers believers *iustitia aliena*, a righteousness not their own; the other *sapientia aliena*, a wisdom not their own. In each letter Paul is asserting with the utmost possible emphasis that salvation is of the Lord, but in each letter he uses a terminology appropriate to the community which he is addressing. Nor is there any doubt that this terminology accurately reflects the language of his original missionary preaching.

Similarly with *didachē*. Both in Matthew and in Luke the Lord's Prayer is found in the context of teaching on prayer (Matt. 6.1–18; Luke 11.1–13), but these two catechisms are designed for quite different communities. The Matthaean catechism is designed for people who have learned to pray but are in danger of misusing prayer, through making a public show of their prayers or heaping up empty phrases. This is Jewish-Christian *didachē*. The Lukan prayer catechism, on the other hand, is directed to people who need to learn to pray and to be encouraged to persist in prayer, in the faith that God will answer. This is Gentile Christian *didachē*.[6]

As for prophecy, this, even more clearly than the other forms of ministry, is related precisely to the situation of this community at this time. The prophetic admonitions contained in Revelation 2 and 3 are all quite specific and quite different. John the Seer could never have written to the church at Laodicea what he writes to the church at Philadelphia or vice versa.

A Word that Transforms

A second characteristic of the ministries of the word reflected in the New Testament is that they are intended not just to inform the hearers but to transform them, directed not just at the intellect but at the will. This is most obviously true of missionary proclamation, which aims at conversion (cf. Acts 2.38; 10.43; 13.38f.; 14.15), and of prophecy, which seeks to move to repentance (Rev. 2.5, 16; 3.3,19), to rekindle faith (3.2,20) and to encourage perseverance (2.10,17,25f.; 3.5,11f.,21), but teaching too is directed not just at the intellect but at the will. We noted in our discussion of parables in Chapter 3 that the parables of Jesus do not represent a didactic linguistic form, which serves the purpose of teaching someone about something, but a rhetorical linguistic form, which seeks to bring about an effect on the hearers. In this respect they can appropriately be compared to jokes. No one tells a joke in the expectation that it will fall flat but in the hope that it will have an effect on the hearers and move them to laughter. In the same way, the parables of Jesus aim at the transformation of the hearers but not primarily in a moral sense. Rather they are addressed first of all to the hearers' imagination and through the imagination to the will. They make present the very thing of which they speak, the kingdom of God, bringing it near to the hearers and inviting them to respond to it now.

The word of God is being scattered abroad with a magnificent prodigality. Let it take root in your heart. Take to heart the message of God's unconditional forgiveness, even though it sounds too good to be true. For now is the day of salvation. The hidden treasure, the pearl of great price, is there for the having. The doors of the Father's house are standing wide open. The invitation to the feast is for you. Now is the moment of decision. Will you not respond with the simplicity of a child?

A Word that is used by God

Now for a further component in the teaching of the New Testament about the various ministries of the word. It has been an essential part of our argument in this chapter that the Christian preacher can claim to stand in the succession of the prophets. The mark of a prophet is that he or she is not simply an expositor of an earlier revelation but the bearer of the living word of God. Thus we find again and again in the New Testament the claim being made that in and through the words of the servants of the word the voice of the Word himself, Jesus Christ, may be heard. The New Testament speaks just as emphatically of a real presence of Christ in the word as it does of a real presence of Christ in the Lord's Supper. 'He who hears you hears me, and he who rejects you rejects me' (Luke 10.16; Matt. 10.40). In the word peace either 'comes upon' a house or 'returns to' the preacher, in which case the house falls under a judgment more terrible than that inflicted on Sodom and Gomorrah (Matt. 10.12–15).[7]

There are three passages in Paul's letters in which this claim is expressed in a particularly striking way. In I Thess. 2.13 Paul reminds his readers of the way in which they received the message he brought them. It is for him a constant occasion for thankfulness to God that when they heard it they accepted it 'not as the word of men but as what it really is, the word of God'. Paul's actual words bring out very clearly the double aspect of their preaching. It had been on the one hand a word of men, mere men, a word the Thessalonians had heard from Paul and his companions, to outward appearance no different from many another travelling orator whom they could hear on the street corners or in the squares of Thessalonica. Moreover, it had been a 'word of men' in the sense of being about men. It spoke of 'one who passed for the son of a carpenter . . . and died like a criminal in the company of robbers'.[8] But the Thessalonians had found in this word something more, they had found themselves addressed by the living, active Word of God.

Equally striking is the claim implicit in Rom. 1.16, where Paul describes the gospel as 'the power of God for salvation to every one who has faith'. For Paul it is not enough to say that the gospel is a rehearsal of the mighty acts (the *dynameis*) of God in the past, though that is certainly true. God had acted for the salvation of men and women, and Christian evangelists like Paul are proclaiming this fact, but this is not all. The gospel is not only the proclamation of a dynamic event; it *is the dynamis*. Paul thinks of the proclamation as being itself a part of the continuing dynamic event. In the proclamation the God who acted in the life, death and resurrection of Jesus is powerfully and savingly present.

The same striking claim is implicit in II Cor. 5.20, where Paul writes, 'So we are ambassadors for Christ, God making his appeal through us. We beseech you on behalf of Christ, be reconciled to God.' As ambassadors for Christ, Paul and other evangelists are his representatives, acting on his behalf, but not as the representatives of one who is absent. On the contrary, through their words of entreaty God himself is making his appeal.

The full force of Paul's words here is muted in the Authorized Version, which translates verse 20, 'Now then we are ambassadors for Christ, as though God did beseech you by us. . . .' The words 'as though', which seem to express doubt whether God actually speaks through the apostles, are used here to translate the Greek word *hōs*. That would be a correct translation if Paul had written *hōs ei*, but he has not. According to a construction common in classical Greek and not uncommon in the New Testament, *hōs* can be used with a participle or a clause to denote the subjective grounds, that is, the reason or intention underlying, or alleged to underlie, the action of the subject of the main verb. This sentence is best understood as an example of that construction. The construction may refer to a genuine reason or intention, as in I Cor. 7.25; or a mere pretext, as in Acts 27.30; a correct belief, as in Heb. 13.17; or a mistaken one, as in Acts 3.12; so that a variety of renderings is called for, such as 'in the belief that', 'while asserting that' or 'under the pretence that'. The one constant element is that the words introduced by *hōs* represent part of the thought of the subject of the verb. The force of the word here is that Paul and his fellow evangelists act as Christ's ambassadors *in the conviction* that God is appealing to men and women through them. There is no suggestion of any doubt whether God is actually speaking through them.[9]

In an essay on Jesus and Paul Bultmann discusses this passage and brings out very clearly how for Paul the saving event, the decisive deed of God in Christ, is made present in preaching, as well as in baptism and eucharist, so that preaching becomes part of the event itself. While outwardly the work of mere men and women, it is also an occasion when Christ is encountered and God speaks.

> The sacraments are celebrations [in which] . . . the unique saving event of the death and resurrection of Christ is made present and actual for the individual and appropriated by him. As the saving event is for Paul the decisive deed of God, which brings the old world to an end and establishes the new world, this event cannot become for him an event of the past like other historical events. It stands, so to speak, outside the flux of time and is valid for all the future as something eternally present. But precisely this eternal presence of the decisive deed of God is appropriated by the individual in baptism and eucharist. . . . But baptism and eucharist are only a particular representation of the saving event, which becomes present in general in the word of preaching. With the cross God has established the office of reconciliation, the word of reconciliation (II Cor. 5.18f.); in other words, the preaching itself belongs to the saving event. It is neither a narrative account about a past event which happened once nor is it instruction about philosophical questions, rather in it one encounters Christ, one is addressed by God himself: 'So therefore in our ministry for Christ God is, so to speak, preaching through our mouth: Be reconciled with God!'[10]

We have been considering three outstanding features of the various ministries of the word found in the New Testament. We noted, first of all, that none of them consists of the repetition of the same message over and over again in the same words. On the contrary, the message is adapted to the particular situation of the hearers. Secondly, all of these forms of ministry are directed not just at the intellect of the hearers but through the intellect and the imagination to the will. Thirdly, these ministries are exercised in the belief that in and through the words of his human servants the voice of the Word, Jesus Christ, will be heard.

A Definition of Preaching

What are the implications of all this for our understanding of preaching? How should we define it? I suggest the following definition: *an act of worship which seeks, in dependence on the presence of God, to bring this passage of scripture, or this aspect of Christian doctrine, to life as a word of importance for the members of this congregation.*[11]

We noted earlier that preaching has evolved over the centuries, so that, as normally practised today, it does not correspond exactly to any one of the various ministries of the word that we read about in the New Testament. Hence the question, 'What is preaching?' cannot be settled by a simple appeal to the Bible. In the end we have to appeal to the church, by putting to it the question, 'This is what we understand by preaching, is it not?' in the hope of initiating a dialogue which will disclose something of a common mind. The definition I have proposed should be understood as an attempt to initiate such a dialogue.

At the same time I derive some support for the definition I have proposed from my own observation of the commonest ways in which church members express the feeling that a sermon has missed the mark. In my experience an expression of disappointment very often takes one or other of the following forms, either 'The preacher didn't really have anything to say', or 'The preacher didn't say anything that was really for me.' In other words, there appears to be a tacit consensus that a sermon should have both substance, – Christian substance, and relevance, – pastoral relevance. The definition proposed attempts to do justice to both those requirements.

Is Preaching Ineffective Pastorally?

Furthermore, if preaching is understood in the way proposed, some common contemporary criticisms of preaching lose their force. Consider, for example, the criticism that preaching fails to meet people's needs, fails to speak to people where they are. One relatively recent diagnosis of the plight of preaching which makes much of this criticism is *The Empty Pulpit* by Clyde Reid. Reid's thesis is that preaching, or at least preaching as we have known it, has had its day. The book is a response to his repeated experience of disappointment with the sermons he was hearing in churches up and down the country at a time when he held a roving commission. Had I myself been present on those occasions, my own sense of disappointment might well have been as keen as his, but I believe I would have drawn a different conclusion. In chapter 2 he devotes two pages to the definition of preaching. Again and again it is defined in terms like these: 'The proclamation of good news, the news of what God has done in history for man, the good news of Jesus Christ.' But if the view of preaching proposed in this chapter is accepted, then any definition of it which does not make explicit reference to this particular congregation is seriously inadequate. Only in his quotation of a statement by Langdon Gilkey does Reid suggest in any way that preaching should be understood as the communication of the gospel to these people at this time. Hence my suspicion that had I been present at the services which caused him so much disappointment I would have drawn a different conclusion. Rather than draw the conclusion, 'This shows that preaching has had its day', I suspect that my verdict would have been, 'This is not true preaching.' No doubt preaching often does fail to speak to people where they are. The remedy, I suggest, is not to abandon preaching altogether but to insist that preaching should be understood as an application of the Christian message to the situation of the hearers – a profoundly pastoral activity.

But if this is accepted, there is an important corollary: preaching, if it is to be effective, cannot be carried out in isolation; it needs to be integrated into a fully pastoral ministry. I suspect that one reason for the disillusionment with preaching expressed by some writers, including perhaps the German author quoted at the beginning of the chapter, is a misconception about the place of preaching within the total ministry, the misconception that good preaching and good preaching alone will guarantee success. To suppose that one can minister adequately to a congregation simply by preaching good sermons is a fallacy. Indeed, it is a fallacy to suppose that one will be able to preach good sermons, if one puts all one's energy into sermon preparation and sits lightly to pastoral work.

This point has been made with disturbing directness by one of the outstanding preachers of this century, Bernard Manning, in an address to the Congregational Union of England and Wales.

> How to interest your people? I cannot tell you. I cannot even describe more than the two or three whom I know. But unless you, to whom the care of Christ's sheep is committed, know what their background is and what their interests are, on what lines their minds and their affections move, you are quite without one half of the material for your sermon. There is an unending task in knowing better and better the minds and hearts of your congregation.[12]

Is Preaching Ineffective Educationally?

Another criticism of preaching that has often been heard in recent years is that it is an ineffective educational technique. Handbooks on Christian Education often contain a diagram called the 'Learning Pyramid', intended to illustrate the effectiveness of different methods of learning, so far as this can be assessed by what is retained by the learner. The gist of the diagram is that people retain only 10% of what they hear and 18% of what they see, whereas the retention level goes up to 50% if verbal and visual experiences are combined, and rises to 80% if they are exposed to simulated experiences, and to 90% if they engage in direct experiences.

If preaching is understood simply as an educational technique designed to communicate information, the conclusion that it is ineffective seems inescapable. But if the argument of this chapter is sound, preaching is something quite different. It is designed not to communicate facts but to humble, to convert and to transform, to enlighten, to

stimulate and to inspire. If this is true, then the question of
how much I can remember of a particular sermon is not of
first importance. The important question is rather, 'Did it
move me? Did it change me?' I myself can still recall being
moved and (I trust) changed by sermons which I heard thirty
or forty years ago and of which I can now remember nothing
but the text, the theme and maybe one illustration. At this
distance the level of verbal retention to which I could lay
claim would be less than 1%, but of the effectiveness of that
preaching there can be no question. I can imagine few things
better fitted to spur preachers on to fresh efforts and to raise
us from satisfaction with our routine performance than the
thought that thirty or forty years hence someone may recall a
sermon of ours with the same gratitude.

So much for the criticism that preaching is an ineffective
educational technique. My response is that this criticism
reflects a misconception of preaching. There is surely also a
great deal more to education than simply the communication of information What about the inculcation of habits or
the teaching of skills? But the appeal to the learning pyramid
focusses attention exclusively on how much is remembered
– a quite inadequate criterion.

Is Preaching Dispensable?

So far we have used each of the first two characteristics of
preaching which we identified earlier in the chapter both as
rejoinders to some criticisms of preaching and as salutary
reminders of what our preaching ought to be. The third
characteristic which we identified, viz. that it is the locus of
the real presence of Christ, can also be used both as a
rejoinder and a salutary reminder. In speaking of it as a
rejoinder I have in mind a criticism which is more often
expressed in actions than in words. I mean the criticism of
preaching implicit, for example, in the actions of church
members who choose to attend 'worship in the round' rather
than a normal service of worship, or in the actions of clergy
who put all their energy into all sorts of alternative
activities: buzz groups, book circles, role playing, encounter
groups, liturgical dance, current affairs seminars, sensitivity

experiences, workshops in neighbouring skills or whatever. I would not for a moment deny that all of these activities have their value, not least because of the opportunity they give the clergy to become acquainted with the background and interests of their parishioners and the lines on which their minds and affections move. It is a different matter when they are seen as substitutes for preaching. Then one has reason to suspect not only a loss of faith in preaching but a loss of faith in the God of the Bible, who precisely in loving, coming, speaking – is God.

There would be less reason to suspect the prevalence of this deeper loss of faith if the enthusiasm for the alternative activities of which I have spoken were normally accompanied by a conviction of the centrality of the Lord's Supper, but in my experience this is not usually so. Conversely, the recovery of a sense of the centrality of the Lord's Supper usually, so far as I have been able to judge, leads to a renewed appreciation of the importance of preaching and vice versa. Indeed these two acts of the church stand or fall together, and what we claim for the one we claim for the other. As we speak of the Lord's Supper as a sacrament, so we may rightly speak of preaching as a sacramental act. As we speak of the real presence of Christ in the Supper, so we may rightly speak of the real presence of Christ in the word of proclamation. Moreover, each action stands in an essential relationship both to the past and to the present. The Lord's Supper is certainly a memorial of Christ, an action done 'in remembrance of me'. But no large Christian community regards the Supper as no more than that, a mere reminder of something that happened a long time ago. The one who gave himself up to death for our sakes gives himself to us now in and through the earthly signs of bread and wine, the words, the sharing, the whole occasion. What we hold to be true of the Supper we also hold to be true of preaching, viz. that the very one to whom we look back gives himself to us afresh in and through the often all-too-earthly words of men and women. The very God who acted in the events to which the Bible bears witness acts afresh in the word of proclamation.

To be sure, the God of whom we speak acts always in sovereign freedom and is never at our disposal. For us to claim to control and manipulate his coming, his speaking, in word and sacrament, would be the height of presumption. Yet it is given to us preachers from time to time to know that our inadequate words have become for someone the vehicle of the Word of God. To such a discovery the only proper response is one of fear and trembling, and the constant prayer that our whole existence may be made so available to him that through us he may continue to speak. And the last thing we will consider doing is abandoning preaching as something that has had its day.

7

From Exegete to Preacher

In the last chapter we addressed ourselves to the questions, 'Why preach?' 'Has preaching had its day?' It now remains for us to reflect on how the transition from exegesis to preaching can best be made.

First of all, however, let it be clearly understood that we are assuming that the preacher will have come to the point of preparing the actual sermon via the road outlined in the first part of this book. Let us therefore briefly recapitulate what this will involve. What are the essential things I need to do by way of exegesis of this passage before I make the deliberate move towards the preparation of a sermon based upon it? And in what order should I do them?

This is a question which has engaged us already, particularly in Chapter 4, where it was argued that the best way to attain a coherent interpretation of a passage is to work consistently from the whole to the parts and back again to the whole. But some of the other conclusions we have reached also bear upon it. For example, the question 'What is the genre to which this passage belongs?' clearly needs to be raised at an early stage. My own judgment is that the procedure which would best do justice to all the theses we have proposed so far would be the following. It does not correspond exactly to the sequence of topics followed in those opening chapters, but that was dictated by the need to justify a method and not simply outline it.

1. I try to make explicit whatever impressions I may have about the dominant concerns of this author, the principal themes of the book to which this passage belongs.[1]

2. I allow the passage as a whole to make its impact upon me, alert to everything which exemplifies the concerns and themes I know to be typical of this author and this book but also alert, or rather with my eyes as wide open as I can force them to anything that is new, unexpected, surprising.[2]

3. I consider the question of the genre to which the passage belongs and what that implies for the way in which I should handle it.[3] At the same time I keep my eyes open to anything which represents a deviation from common literary patterns.[4]

4. I explore the passage in greater and greater detail,[5] asking myself what are the theological problems with which it is concerned,[6] reflecting on its history and on the use which the author has made of the materials at his disposal,[7] filling out my understanding of the theologically significant words.[8]

5. I work towards a grasp of the meaning of the passage as a whole, attentive to any ways in which my provisional understanding of the author's concerns in this passage has been modified by more detailed study.[9] I try to picture the sort of readers he had in mind and to state succinctly in my own words what he was trying to communicate to them.[10]

6. Remembering that the author may have said, and may have been perceived as saying, more than he was aware of, I watch out for barely conscious meanings in the text, as well as subconscious meanings. I ask myself whether the passage acquires a new depth in the light of the author's total work, or a new level of meaning in the light of the total biblical witness, and whether it shines in a new light through being read in a new life-setting. I also ask whether, in the light of the total biblical witness, it calls for some sort of qualification.[11]

Too Rigid?

I am well aware that some readers will resist the idea of a procedure containing no fewer than six steps. Why, you may ask, be tied to such a rigid method? I would argue that, paradoxical though it may seem, such a method enables you to retain the initiative for your project in your own hands. If you begin by plunging into commentaries, dictionaries, articles and monographs, you will inevitably be conditioned by their interests and their method. There is also a real risk that you will be swamped by details and unable to see the wood for trees. And, in the desire to do justice to the breadth of your reading, you may end up by making no more than a compilation. But, if you follow one by one the steps I have outlined, your mind will be alert at each stage to a precise objective.

There is, in fact, a great deal to be said for beginning by working through the various steps, using no other tools than a Greek text and a translation. However rudimentary such a first draft may be, it is invaluable as a way of sensitizing you to the text and ensuring that your work will carry the stamp of your own individuality. Then you can turn to the commentaries with a clearer idea of the questions to which you are seeking an answer and read them through more rapidly.

Fixed or Flexible?

In recommending a particular order, however, I do not wish to suggest in any way that it is the only right one. For example, the best first step may well be to allow the passage as a whole to make its impact upon you, to let it speak. On the other hand, I do not regard the question of order as a trivial one or as a matter of purely personal taste. Every preacher must answer for himself or herself, but my experience has been that when a sermon costs me an inordinate amount of labour the reason very often proves to be, on reflection, that I have followed an inappropriate order in my preparation – like thinking up an outline of a sermon and then looking around for a text on which to base it.

The Next Step

So far, then, the minister as exegete. All of the steps I have outlined so far could be followed equally well by a student preparing an exegetical exercise as by a minister preparing for a Sunday service. But what next? How do I build a bridge from text to sermon? How do I move most responsibly from exegesis to preaching?

In what follows I am going to outline one method only. Again, however, I do not wish to suggest in any way that it is only by following this method that one can preach responsibly or even preach biblically. As John Knox has observed, it is possible to preach a quite biblical sermon on no text at all, just as it is possible to preach a quite unbiblical sermon on a biblical text, by quoting a few words as a kind of ornamental frontispiece for a discourse which really owes nothing either to those words or to any other part of the Bible.[12]

The most glaring example of such a misuse of a text known to me comes from a collection of sermons by one Archibald Alexander. For one sermon he chose as his text Hos. 7.9, in its context a telling description of the blinding effects of sin, of how a people can become so steeped in sin that in the end they lose the awareness of their own sinfulness. Verses 8 and 9 read:

> Ephraim is a cake not turned. Aliens devour his strength, and he knows it not; grey hairs are sprinkled upon him, and he knows it not.

The theme of Alexander's sermon is 'Growing old gracefully'.[13]

John Knox's definition of what constitutes truly biblical preaching is well worth pondering. According to Knox, biblical preaching is, first, preaching which is centrally concerned with the central biblical event, the event of Christ; secondly, preaching which seeks to be faithful to the characteristic and essential biblical ideas; thirdly, preaching which answers to, and nourishes, the essential life of the church, and, fourthly, preaching in which the event which is proclaimed is in a real sense recurring.[14]

It would be presumptuous to suggest that such preaching can only be carried out by following one method of preparation. All that I would claim for the method of sermon preparation which I am about to expound is that it is consistent with the principles of biblical interpretation proposed in the first part of this book.

Our starting-point is something which I stressed particularly in Chapter 2, viz. that the writings of the New Testament are all deeply pastoral and therefore conspicuously intentional writings. Their authors are not writing simply in order to gratify a creative impulse for the benefit of anyone who may care to read. They are writing out of deep pastoral concern for specific communities of believers and seeking to speak to their needs.

This is a point which is particularly stressed by Willi Marxsen and Leander Keck. Marxsen never tires of insisting that the writings of the Bible are, with only one or two exceptions, communications (*Aussagen*) between a writer and a particular circle of readers. He also speaks of their essential 'directedness' (*Gerichtetheit*).[15] Similarly Keck writes that essentially the Bible is a collection of occasional literature, by which he does not mean literature that is written for special occasions but literature that is 'occasioned by', that is, 'elicited by particular occasions or situations in the life of the communities of faith'.[16]

If this view of the biblical writings is accepted, then it has important implications for preaching. The texts with which we are dealing do not consist of a series of timeless statements of faith and timeless principles of conduct to which we have somehow to tack on an application that relates them to our own situation. On the contrary, they are already by way of being an application of the gospel, so that our task is rather to let them be heard afresh and to let them resonate with our own experience. From this it follows that the kind of preaching which accords most closely with the intention of the biblical authors will be that which addresses itself to a situation or need comparable to that which they themselves were addressing. This means that as I begin to move from the exegesis of the passage to the sermon proper I ask myself, 'When have I or my people stood somewhere near where those people were standing to whom this passage was originally directed and felt something like what they were feeling?' (This represents Step 7.)

It is all too easy for a preacher to move too quickly to the application of a text to today's congregation and thereby fail to respect the particularity of the situation of the original readers. One suspects that this premature move is being made when one hears the preacher say 'Paul says to us . . .' or 'Paul says to the Galatians and to us. . . .' But Paul was not speaking to us. He was speaking to the Galatians, or maybe the Philippians or Philemon. It may well be that what he said to them also has something to say to us, but that is a quite different question.

To take another example: in the third chapter of Revelation we find, among other things, these three statements.

'I know your works; you have the name of being alive, and you are dead' (3.1b).

'I know that you have but little power, and yet you have kept my word and have not denied my name' (3.8b).

'I know your works: you are neither cold nor hot. Would that you were cold or hot! So, because you are lukewarm, I will spew you out of my mouth' (3.15f.).

It would be irresponsible for a preacher to fasten on one of these texts and say 'John the Seer says to his readers and to us, "I know your works: you are neither cold nor hot. . .".' The three statements quoted above are in fact from three different letters to three different churches in three different situations. Each statement is addressed to this particular community. It is a word that strikes home for them in their situation and is applicable to us only insofar as our situation is comparable to theirs.

But may we speak of their situation being comparable to ours? Between those original readers and ourselves lie nearly twenty centuries. Surely an historical distance of that magnitude needs to be taken with the utmost seriousness? Indeed, but it is my conviction that it is usually possible, while respecting the distance, to find a situation in our own lives which is comparable to that of the original readers, a correspondence that is real and not strained or artificial.

It should be noted that we are not claiming that it is usually possible to find a situation that is identical, though that will happen sometimes. If the text is taken from I Corinthians 14 and the congregation to which I am to preach is one which sets great store by speaking in tongues, then I will be able to speak of an essential identity between the situation of Paul's readers and that of my hearers. However, a comparable, if not identical, situation will usually suggest itself. By way of illustration, let us consider some of the books which have already been discussed in earlier chapters.

In Chapter 2 it was suggested that John 21 points to the situation of John's primary readers being that of people for whom Jesus was in danger of becoming more and more remote.[17] It appears that the Beloved Disciple, the leader of their community and their principal living link with Jesus, has just died, leaving them feeling orphaned and bereft. At the same time the expectation of Jesus's imminent return has proved to be mistaken. In these circumstances there is a real danger of them losing a sense of the living presence of Jesus in the here and now. They have the memory of the Jesus who came (now receding further and further into the past) and the hope of the Jesus who is to come (now disappearing further and further into the future) but for the present a sense of emptiness. If such was their situation, then it is not wholly alien to our experience, for all of us have known times when Jesus seemed to be becoming more and more remote.

In Chapter 4 it was suggested that Luke, in telling the story of the spread of the gospel from Jerusalem to the ends of the earth, is particularly concerned to address Christians who are looking wistfully over their shoulders and wondering ruefully whether the Gentile Mission, which has led to the final separation between church and synagogue, has not been a great mistake.[18] Again, I find no difficulty in recalling times when I myself and the people to whom I minister have wondered whether our church, in taking some major action of outreach, may not, however praiseworthy its conscious intentions, have made a great mistake.

It was suggested in the same chapter that in the last two chapters of I Thessalonians Paul is addressing a community of people who, since his departure, have had to undergo painful experiences for which they were not fully prepared and, as a result, are beginning to wonder about the reality of their first experience with the gospel.[19] Again it is surely not difficult for any of us to recall a comparable experience.

The spiritual condition of the first readers of the letter to the Hebrews was discussed in some detail in Chapter 2.[20] We found there good reason to describe it as a condition of faith-fatigue. The readers have got stuck at an elementary level of understanding; they are in need of milk when they should be having solid food. They are also in danger of losing heart, of collapsing before the finishing post. This is a spiritual condition which is all too familiar throughout the churches of the Western world.

In the same chapter we noted some of the problems with which Revelation presents the interpreter, both in its totality and in respect to individual visions.[21] It is not difficult, however, to feel a real affinity with the questioning state of mind to which the author is addressing himself. Which of us, while reading about some catalogue of horrors in the newspaper or watching it portrayed on television, has not sometimes asked himself, 'What is God doing in this world of ours? What on earth is he up to in all this?' That is essentially the state of mind to which apocalyptic, for all the bizarreness of its imagery, is directed.

From identifying what my hearers have in common with the author's original readers it is but a short step to a redirection of the meaning intended by the author so as to let it speak to my hearers. (This I shall call Step 8.) It has been maintained throughout this book that the writers of the New Testament, in addressing specific communities, specific circles of readers, sought to speak to their needs. The message matches the audience and acquires a sharper point, the more clearly we are able to visualize their situation. It is a word that strikes home for them in their situation. Paul would never have written to the Philippians what he wrote to the Galatians, or *vice versa*. But if I can identify in myself or among my hearers a condition comparable to that addressed by the original author, I can surely also restate the message he was seeking to convey to his audience in such a way that it becomes a word that strikes home for mine. Thus to those for whom Jesus seems to be becoming more and more remote I can retell the story of the healing of the son of the royal official in such a way as to communicate to them something of John's conviction that the word of Jesus is a word that brings life; and that through faith, faith which trusts his word, faith which trusts without seeing, the life which is his gift may still be had.

Or if I have identified as something which my hearers have in common with Luke's first readers the fear that our church, in attempting to reach out, has taken a wrong turning, I can invite them to listen with Luke's readers as he tells 'the story of the minute but mighty mustard seed',[22] the 'chosen vessel', which neither storm nor shipwreck, neither the plotting of evil men nor the attack of the serpent, can prevent from achieving God's design.

Or, if the text for the day comes from I Thessalonians 1 or 2, I can invite my hearers to picture a community of new converts wondering about the reality of their first experience with the gospel because of unexpected setbacks which they have experienced, to recall the times when they themselves have stood where Paul's first readers stood and then to hear anew Paul's ringing assurance that the message he had brought was 'for real', the very word of God himself.

Or, if the text comes from Hebrews, then I have the opportunity to show how the writer of that letter responded to the signs of faith-fatigue among the communities for which he was concerned, a malaise only too familiar to us, by seeking to impart to them a deeper understanding of the work of Christ.

Before we move from the exposition of this method of sermon preparation to critical reflection upon it, I make two comments by way of clarification.

First, up till now I have made a careful distinction between the question how the text spoke to its first readers back there and the question how it might speak to us today. Nicholas Lash, however, argues that while that distinction is a convenient one, there is in fact an intimate dialectical relationship between the two questions. If we are to understand, with any depth and sensitivity, what a biblical text meant, we need a clear grasp of those fundamental features of the human predicament to which the author was responding. 'If', he writes 'the questions to which ancient authors sought to respond . . . are to be "heard" today with something like their original force and urgency, they have first to be "heard"

as questions that challenge us with comparable seriousness. . . . There is thus a sense in which the articulation of
what the text might "mean" today is a necessary condition
of hearing what that text "originally meant".'23

It should further be noted that the use of the method need
not be limited to those occasions when I am able to identify
among my hearers a condition comparable to that addressed
by the original writer. At times indeed the danger will be that
they will find the text only too congenial through failing to
notice that their own situation does not exactly correspond
to that of the original readers. If so, then my task will be to
make this clear and show how a responsible application of
the passage to their situation must necessarily involve a
change of emphasis.

For example, the main thrust of I Corinthians 14 is to
direct the attention of Paul's readers away from speaking in
tongues towards gifts of the Spirit which are of more value for
building up the congregation. That was the emphasis which
Paul felt called upon to make when writing to the Corinthians, who evidently conceived of the Spirit as a gift which
lifted them, or rather lifted the favoured few, the 'spiritual
ones', right out of this world. But suppose that the congregation which I am addressing is an excessively cerebral one, all
too prone to pour scorn on any signs of spiritual enthusiasm.
In preaching to such a congregation a wooden reproduction
of the emphasis of I Corinthians 14 would be inappropriate
and indeed inconsistent with Paul's purpose. In such a
situation I would be entirely justified in giving the fullest
weight to the positive statements about the more dramatic
gifts of the Spirit which Paul allows himself to make. But we
must now move towards more explicit critical reflection
upon the method.

A Word that is Specific

First, it should by now be clear how, through the exploration
of certain precise questions – To whom is this author
writing? When have I or my people stood somewhere near to
where they were standing? What is this author seeking to
communicate to his audience? What might that mean for

mine? – the outlines of a sermon can begin to open up. It will
also be apparent that the preacher who follows this method
of sermon preparation will not address his or her congregation in a general way but will speak to a definite situation, a
particular spiritual condition, a particular need, a particular
trial of faith. Is that a defect? I do not think so. Too many
sermons that I have heard, as well as not a few that I have
preached, have been addressed to no one in particular and, as
a result, have had no sharp point, no cutting edge.

The need for such a cutting edge is seen as all the more
urgent, once one realizes how easily the mere act of listening
to the Bible in a liturgical setting can have a soporific effect,
much like the effect of listening to a fairy tale. We are caught
up into a story which removes us from the everyday world.
There is a certain simplification; our world is reduced to a
manageable stage. Furthermore, the world of the biblical
story has a certain romance about it – kings, high priests and
the like. As H. H. Farmer has observed, the very desire of the
preacher to evoke the past in a picturesque and interesting
way and so hold the hearer's attention may create an
impression of unreality. He writes:

> The scene comes before the listener almost like a costume
> or period play, on the background of an advertisement of
> the P. and O. line – blue sky, white walls, robed figures and
> all the glamour of the mysterious East. How big the jump
> to the dirty flatness of the wet street on Monday morning,
> waiting for the bus by the mean little pub at the corner, the
> drab monotony, the long littleness, the mechanised fixity
> of factory work![24]

What is more, the world of the Bible is a world in which
things happen that we only dream about. Crippled hands are
made well. Blind eyes recover their sight. The hungry receive
bread and fish. Storms are stilled. In controversies Jesus
always knows the right answer, and in the parables he always
speaks to the hearts of his hearers. In this way the Bible can
become for us a counter-world, in which our dreams at last
find fulfilment, a world foreign to reality, which does not
touch the lives we are actually living. If this miasma of
unreality is to be dispelled, however, we need to hear a clear

word that impinges on our everyday lives and speaks to an aspect of our actual human condition.

It is true that by giving the sermon a sharp point we may leave some of our hearers feeling that we are not speaking directly to something which they themselves have already experienced, but the operative word here is 'already'. All preachers worth their salt know how difficult it is to say something directly relevant to every member of a congregation. It is inevitable that what one says should bear more directly on those people whose needs one has on one's heart at that moment. Yet it should not require a great effort of imagination on the part of our hearers to realize that the need to which we are speaking may one day be theirs. It may indeed already be theirs but still be awaiting their recognition, and may be brought to their consciousness through reflection upon a condition which at first sight seems strange to them.

In any case, we do our hearers a disservice, if we encourage them to believe that the process of applying the text to their situation is wholly our task and not one in which they too are to share. The most effective advertising is very often not that which hammers home its point but that which invites the viewer to draw a deduction. So it is with preaching.

The Need for Depth

By way of further critical reflection upon the method, we may now recall the complaint of many pastors and students, noted in Chapter 2, that when they engage intensively with a text, using the historical-critical method, they often find little that is of any use for preaching or the practice of ministry in general. Part of the answer to this problem lies, I believe, in focussing one's exegesis more deliberately on the situation of the original readers and trying to penetrate below the surface. On the surface the questions troubling the Thessalonians, for example, may appear to have little in common with ours, but their basic situation, that of having experienced unexpected setbacks after their first liberating encounter with the gospel, is by no means alien.

It will by now be clear that I wish to stress the continuities between our world and the world of the Bible much more strongly than is done by Ernest Best in his book, *From Text to Sermon*. Best argues that our culture, many of our situations and much of our world view are different from those of the New Testament. What preachers tend to do, when the passage on which they wish to preach deals with a situation bound up with the culture of the first century, is to look for an equivalent situation and try to translate into that situation what Paul has been saying. But, he adds, when the translation is analysed, it is usual to find that the parallel situation is no true parallel and when pushed breaks down. As an example of such a first-century situation which resists translation into a modern equivalent he cites the problem of meat offered to idols.[25]

This is the sort of issue which divided first-century Christians into two camps, according as they took an emancipated or an ultra-scrupulous line. In Rom. 14.1–15.6 Paul characterizes these two camps as the strong and the weak. The issues over which they were divided, issues of food and abstinence and holy days, are indeed remote from us, but the attitudes which the division generated are far from being remote. 'Let not him who eats despise him who abstains, and let not him who abstains pass judgment on him who eats' (Rom. 14.3). The emancipated Christian is in danger of yielding to contempt, the overscrupulous Christian in danger of yielding to censoriousness. These are not temptations peculiar to the first century; they have, on the contrary, an uncomfortably familiar ring. But this only becomes apparent when we explore thoroughly the situation of the people whom Paul is addressing and try to penetrate below the surface.

In the same way, our exegesis is more likely to prove fruitful for preaching if we can penetrate below the level of the text and focus on the author's underlying intention. To use as an example a passage not yet quoted, there is in I Peter 3.19f. an initially strange allusion to Christ preaching after his crucifixion to the spirits in prison who had proved disobedient in the days of Noah. But the passage becomes luminous with meaning once it is realized that the people of Noah's generation were proverbial in contemporary Jewish literature for their ungodliness. The passage is thus a striking expression of the universality of the offer of grace. For the writer and his readers the generation of Noah were the prototypes of all sinners, and yet salvation is open even to them. So the scope of Christ's saving activity is such that we dare not set any limits to it; even the most seemingly hopeless sinners are not incapable of redemption through him.

If we but dig deep enough, we will find again and again a message that resonates with our own experience. It is true that the particularity of the historical situation of the first readers of the New Testament writings needs to be respected, as does the particularity of our own historical situation. It is true that between them and us there lie nearly twenty centuries. It may even be true to say, as Best does, that our culture, many of our situations and much of our world view are different from all of those of the New Testament.[26] But it is also true that we find mirrored in the New Testament temptations, frailties and needs which are only too familiar to us, so that we can recognize those original readers as bone of our bone and flesh of our flesh. Then, to adapt Karl Barth's words, the walls which separate the twentieth century from the first become transparent. Paul speaks, and the man or woman of the twentieth century hears.[27]

I gladly find support for this position from the concluding remarks of David Daiches in *God and the Poets*, in which he argues that the appreciation of poetry written in ages other than our own would be impossible if some common human factor were not involved. Yet we know that readers can and do achieve such an appreciation.

> Yes, he writes, there are great differences between post-industrial Western society and the societies that preceded it. . . But the basic nature of the human predicament remains, and there comes a point at which we can respond with moving recognition to the poetic expression of an aspect of that predicament, from however alien a culture it may have emanated.[28]

But what if, in spite of all this community of experience, a contemporary situation or spiritual state comparable to that addressed by the original author does not suggest itself? What then?

When Contemporary Parallels Fail

First of all let us note that when we are dealing with a passage from the Synoptic Gospels the question, 'To whom was this passage originally addressed?' often admits of several answers. In the examples already cited we have consistently directed our attention to the readers addressed by the final author, but let us suppose we are dealing with a parable. We could equally well direct our attention further back to the Christian community for whose benefit the parable was preserved and transmitted or, further back still, to the actual situation in the ministry of Jesus in which it was first told. However, it is not always possible to find an answer to the questions of audience at each one of these levels. For example, while we can see signs of the tradition concerning the Lord's Prayer having served a specific purpose in the community behind Matthew and in the community behind Luke, we simply do not know under what circumstances Jesus himself taught it. Besides, even if we could identify three different audiences to which a parable was directed at different stages of its transmission, it is conceivable that we might have difficulty in identifying ourselves with any one of them. What then?

It will then be necessary to concentrate on the passage as a text rather than as a communication between this author and these readers. It may be that, as I reflect on the essential ideas of the passage in themselves, a possible homiletical development begins to take shape. One danger of this approach is that the sermon which results may be addressed to no one in particular and, while it may contain some interesting ideas, have no sharp point, no cutting edge.

Consider, for example, Romans 6. What pastoral concern led Paul to introduce this section into the argument of the letter? To whom in particular is he speaking here? Presumably to people to whom he has been slanderously reported to be exhorting believers to do evil so that good may come, or at least to be preaching a gospel which lent itself to the drawing of that conclusion (cf. Rom. 3.8).

It may well be that none of us has ever been in a situation identical with that or even comparable with it. What then is the essential thrust of the passage in itself? Is it not that baptism involves a sharing in Christ's death and resurrection, a sharing which is understood in a profoundly ethical way as a dying to sin and being set upon our feet with the freedom to walk in newness of life? It may well be that this moment of personal renewal in Paul's understanding of the gospel has received scant attention in our own teaching and thinking about the Christian life, in proportion to the emphasis we have given to forgiveness or justification, and that we have at times preached what Bonhoeffer called a 'gospel of cheap grace'.[29] If so, an appropriate homiletic application of the passage should not be difficult to make.

Or again the best way for me to arrive at an effective homiletic application of a passage may be to take a wider view, and to pursue further the questions I have already asked myself as exegete when I considered whether the passage acquires new levels of meaning or demands to be qualified in some way, when read in the context of the Bible as a whole. To take this broader view of a passage can be very fruitful and is also not without its dangers. Sometimes a single phrase seems to light up with meaning because it encapsulates the essence of the author's thought or, it may be, the thought of another biblical author. I have long held the view, for instance, that five words found in Jonah 2.9 capture the heart of Paul's gospel. In the Authorized Version these words read, 'Salvation is of the Lord'.[30]

Again I can recall a colleague of mine preaching an extremely effective sermon at an ordination service on the text, 'Silver and gold have I none; but such as I have give I thee: in the name of Jesus Christ of Nazareth rise up and walk' (Acts 3.6). The gist of the sermon was that what the Christian minister has to offer is, in the end, nothing tangible, nothing but a bare word, but a word which has the power to set people on their feet and enable them to walk in newness of life. What made the sermon so effective for me was partly its appropriateness to the occasion and partly the way it seemed to sum up so much of the argument of II Corinthians, where Paul finds himself compelled to vindicate his apostleship in the face of rivals who could boast of gifts of personality and oratory far more spectacular than his. In response to the charge that his bodily presence is weak and his speech contemptible (II Cor. 10.10), Paul can only point to what Christ has done for his converts through the message which he had brought (II Cor. 3.2f.). For me and (I know) for many others, the sermon at that ordination service was an example of truly biblical preaching, 'biblical' because of its fidelity to characteristic and essential biblical ideas, and 'preaching' because it was a word that struck home for the people whom the preacher was addressing. Whenever a text seems to light up in this way with a meaning reaching far beyond its immediate context, we need to be sure that those two conditions are, or can be, met, instead of moving immediately to the composition of a sermon.

When Biblical Parallels Fail

In our critical reflection on the method of sermon preparation which we are proposing, we have considered the possibility that we may not be able to find a contemporary situation or spiritual state comparable to that addressed by the original author. But there is also another way in which our situation not only may differ from that of the first readers but does differ. As Best has shown, some of our most pressing problems are due to technological advances which the Bible in no way anticipated.[31] If we therefore limit our use of the Bible to applying it to situations in our experience which are in some way comparable to those of the Bible's first readers, there is a danger that important areas of modern life will be left untouched. This means that the method of sermon preparation which I am proposing is not suited for constant use. But that is not what I want to suggest anyway.

A Direct Word?

As for those occasions when there seems to be no modern counterpart to the situation of the biblical addressees, I have suggested that the preacher's best strategy in such circumstances is either to concentrate on the passage as text rather than as communication or to view it in the context of the Bible as a whole or both. Some readers may well feel, however, that even this modification of the original method is still too restrictive and does not allow sufficiently for the guidance of the Spirit.

That the role of the preacher in preaching is a strictly subordinate and ancillary one we would not for a moment deny. In the foreword to one of his volumes of sermons Eduard Schweizer defines the preacher's task as being that of perceiving what God is seeking to say through the text to the present situation of the hearer.[32]

Note that he refers to what *God* is seeking to say. That is why preaching is a prophetic vocation. That is also why Schweizer stresses so strongly that the preacher's role is a strictly subordinate one. The preacher is a mere translator, one who stands alongside the real speaker, God; a mere midwife, helping something to come to birth.

But this does not mean that all that the preacher needs to do is sit and wait for God to tell him what to say. To be sure, our aim and prayer, first, last and all the time, is that through our words God's word may be heard, but the God to whose word we seek to offer a voice, however haltingly, is the one who stands behind *this text* – that, surely, is what the doctrine of inspiration means in essence – and, further, the one who is seeking to speak *through* it to the present situation of our hearers – that is what it means to say that the Bible contains the word of God. We must ever be ready for God in his freedom to short-circuit our methods of sermon preparation, including the method outlined in this book, and speak directly to our condition, but the word that is thus given to us will bring with it, if it is a genuine word from God, a deeper understanding of the biblical text.

We turn now to the two final stages of the process of preparation which I am outlining.

It may well be thought that the process, as outlined so far, is already long enough. Why introduce two further steps? Simply because I regard them as indispensable if our preaching is to be fully effective. So to Step 9.

Having reflected upon the essential thrust of the passage, both in its immediate context and in the wider context of the

Bible, I then ask myself, 'Why do I believe this to be a word of importance for the lives of these people?'

The Witness of the Heart

There are two reasons why I consider this cluster of questions to be indispensable, if our preaching is to be fully effective. The first is that it opens up a conversation not only between the text and myself as exegete but between the text and myself as person, and thereby shifts the whole exercise from the level of the head to the level of the heart.[33]

A major emphasis of the last chapter was that preaching should be designed not just to inform but to transform, directed not just at the intellect of the hearers but through the intellect, the feelings and the imagination at the will. In other words, it is an exercise in persuasion. But it will not be fully persuasive unless my hearers feel that I am totally behind what I am saying, meeting them not just as a teacher, expounding some ideas that are of interest to me, but as a witness, witnessing with my whole being to what I am saying. But if I am to do that, I must know that this is something which I believe and I must know why I believe it, why I still believe it and still wish to affirm it, in spite of whatever there may be that seems to speak against it.

This is not to say that I should not preach until I have reached a state of serene certitude, totally immune to doubt. By attaining to such a state of serenity I would become not better qualified to preach to others but worse qualified. My hearers would feel that I was no longer bone of their bone and flesh of their flesh. The minister is a person representatively set apart, but that does not mean that he or she is to be a person set aloof.[34]

Nor does it detract from the force of a sermon if it becomes apparent, even as I am preaching, that I still feel the force of the things that seem to speak against what I am affirming. On the contrary, my hearers will be the more open to what I am affirming if they perceive that I am not immune to trials of faith and that the difficulties and doubts which they know are mine too. As John Baillie has observed, many of the greatest defences of the faith have been constructed by people who were obviously arguing with their own difficulties and doubts, whether past (because the answer had already been found) or present (because the answer was only now being worked out with labour and tears), so that in constructing them they were as much concerned to fortify their own souls as to confound their adversaries.

> Seldom, he writes, has a Christian affirmation been effectively defended by one who had no personal feeling for the difficulty of maintaining it and the force of the exception which might be taken to it. The most moving and persuasive arguments are always those in which the arguer is felt to be holding high debate with himself.[35]

That is why a conversation must be opened up not only between the text and myself as exegete but between the text and myself as person.

Leander Keck has drawn a valuable distinction between *listening in on* the conversation between the biblical writer and his original readers, on the one hand, and *listening to it*, on the other. 'One begins to listen to the text', he writes, 'when one is drawn into the discussion, when one must deal with the subject matter, engage its theme and in effect begin conversing with the text and its author.'[36] Clearly the effort to *listen to* a text is not merely an intellectual exercise but rather a matter of letting the text speak to me as a person, a thinking, feeling, willing person, a believer, but a believer who must continue to pray, 'Lord, I believe, help my unbelief.'

The Witness of Tradition

The second reason why we need to probe as deeply as we can the truth of any message we are considering preaching is that such probing opens up a conversation not only between myself and the author or even between myself and the Bible but between myself and the whole Christian tradition of reflection and experience. If I am able to affirm with conviction the main thrust of this text, it will be, in part, because it is of a piece with what I have found compelling in other writings which I have read over the years and with what I know to have been part of the faith by which earlier generations of Christians have lived. I may well discover that the main thrust of the text is an expression of something quite central to Christian thought and experience over the centuries. Such a discovery can hardly fail to strengthen my conviction of the truth of the message I have found in the text and thereby make my own preaching the more convincing.

I stress particularly the importance of Christian experience through the centuries. The Bible itself impels us to look for a witness to its truth in the continuing history of the people of God, for the one of whom it speaks is the living God, the partner of human history from generation to generation, 'The same yesterday, today and for ever.' What God has done or declared once has a truth which is continually renewed. The God of the exodus is continually proving himself anew in the history of his people in biblical times to be the exodus God (see Ps. 78; 114; Isa. 31.5; 43.16– 21; 52.12; I Cor. 5.7). And therefore surely in the ongoing life of his people right down to our own time. But, if so, these texts cannot be confined to the past; they speak of a reality which cannot be so confined. As Chevallier puts it, there is in them a kind of hermeneutical spring projecting the meanings which past generations have found in them towards new meanings to be discovered in the present.[37]

Not Without Anguish

But such discoveries are not made without hard work and real heartsearching. Let us recall once more some of the passages which I used as examples earlier in the chapter. If I am preaching on John 4.46–54, I must ask myself, 'Do I believe that the word of Jesus is a word that brings life; and that through faith, faith which trusts his word, faith which trusts without seeing, the life which is his gift may still be had?' If preaching on Acts, I must ask myself, 'Do I believe that the church is God's chosen vessel, still used by him for the furtherance of his saving purposes, in spite of its own infidelities and the hostility and indifference of the secular world?' Or if preaching from I Thessalonians 1 or 2, I must ask myself, 'Do I still believe that the word which first brought me to faith was "for real", the very word of God himself?' As I struggle with questions like these, I shall be driven back to the Bible again and again but not only to the Bible; the resources on which I may draw will be as wide as my knowledge of literature, as wide as my knowledge of church history, as wide as my experience of life. At any moment a spark may jump between the biblical text and my own knowledge and experience so that each throws light on the other.

To bring a biblical text to bear upon the totality of our experience in the way I have described will call for a real effort on our part, if we have been conditioned by our training to distancing ourselves to some extent from the text, to treating it as an object for cool, impartial, clinical study, but all great imaginative literature cries out for appreciation at a deeper level than the purely cerebral. Any preacher, and any biblical scholar, would do well to ponder Alice Hadfield's account of how Charles Williams, the close friend of C. S. Lewis and J. R. R. Tolkien and a significant author in his own right, succeeded in communicating his enthusiasm for poetry to his evening class students.

> Poetry was related to fundamental experience. It lived by experience and experience lived, or was understood, more fully in poetry. The griefs and glories in poetry are the griefs and glories by which every man's mind lives, the clerk, the shop-assistant, the housewife. The only requirement, as in all heavenly things, is desire, and a mind which takes seriously what poetry says and the conclusions it arrives at, questioning, examining, protesting, but never, never detached. It was this simplicity of becoming involved, this lack of a cunning withdrawal from personal commitment, which C. W. had found in his evening-class students, and did not so easily find among more intellectual people. . .
> He often remarked that it was harder for the man rich in culture to coinhere with the kingdom than for any number of camels to thread themselves through needles.
>
> He would have felt with Jean Paul Sartre in the first chapter of *What is Literature?* where Sartre writes of the literary critics who have 'found a quiet little job as cemetery

watchmen'. Bookshelves of the classics are to them stacks of urns in a columbarium. To them a book is not 'an act nor even a thought. Written by a dead man about dead things, . . . it speaks of nothing which interests us directly.' In it there is mention of passions which the critic does not feel, of anger without object, of fears and hopes that are dead. To the critic and intellectual it is a disembodied world, beautiful and unreal, which does not touch their grievances and anxieties, but is a matter for analysis, for balanced periods, for sensitive and noble funeral rites.

It was not so that C. W.'s students were to read poetry. It was not to be a 'subject', a matter for analysis, comparison, arrangement, or even explanation, anyway not until we were far, far more deeply in it. The existential attitude operated here as strongly as towards love, or God. We were to attend to what poetry is about, and how that concerned our own lives. In this again he developed the idea that Sartre uses in *What is Literature?* when he says that what the writer requires of the reader is 'the gift of his whole person, with his passions, his prepossessions, his sympathies, his sexual temperament, and his scale of values'. . .

The great poets can be almost killed for the reader by the weight of criticism, but C.W.'s touch restores them to us. Never mind whether this scene comes out of an earlier play by another hand, never mind if this passage shows the authoritarian decay of his thought – that can come in a footnote – here is murder, here is the soul destroying itself, here is the first turn of the mind to good, here, in these dozen lines, if you can bear it, is the very life of joy.[38]

The Form

And so, finally, to the form of presentation. I have worked through the various exegetical steps. I have tried to grasp the intention of the biblical author in relation to his original readers. I have alerted myself to the possibility of the text yielding further levels of meaning in the light of the total biblical context and the life-setting within which I am reading it. I have asked myself how this message might be redirected so as to speak to my hearers. I have struggled with the question of its truth. And now, I trust, I have found something that I want, above all, to say. A word has grasped me which is compelling, which demands to be preached. But how do I say it?

First, I will by now have to hand an abundance of material. By identifying within this material a message which is crying out to be preached, I will already have begun a process of selection. Clearly I will need to continue that process and then arrange and present what I have selected in the way that is likely to be most effective.

It is also clearly important that I should catch and hold the attention of my hearers. The surest way of doing that is to make it clear from the outset that what I have to say concerns them, that is, to make contact with life as they have experienced it. The late Helmut Rex, Professor of Church History at Knox College, Dunedin, used to speak with feeling to his students about the 'when-the-Israelites-left-Egypt type of sermon, which drags the hearer for twenty minutes from Dan to Beersheba'.

I will already have asked myself, 'When have my people stood closest to the readers whom the author was addressing?' If an answer has suggested itself, I can make that my starting-point. 'Have you ever wondered, as you read the paper or watched the news on television, "What on earth is God doing in the world at the present time?" ' From there a natural next step would be to show how that question was a burning one for the first readers of Revelation, then show how John the Seer sought to speak to their need and finally relate the essential thrust of his message to those anxieties of ours which lead us to ask the same urgent question as the original readers of Revelation.

But it may also be possible to involve the congregation more actively in the process of reflecting on the meaning of the biblical text and its application to our own lives. I might, for example, sketch the pastoral situation which occasioned the writing in question and then ask the congregation to consider in small groups in what ways their own situation is comparable with that of the first readers. Hebrews, let us say, was addressed to people suffering from faith-fatigue, a faith-fatigue expressed in this way and in that. Is this a state with

which we are familiar? Discuss. From there I could proceed
to show how the author of Hebrews tried to speak to the
situation of his readers and then relate the essential thrust of
his message to faith-fatigue as we know it.

Scope for Dialogue

But at this latter point it may well be possible to involve my
hearers once again in a more active way. Why not invite
them to consider how they might make their own the
essential thrust of the passage, instead of performing the
whole process by myself? To be sure, as we saw earlier in this
chapter, more is involved in the effective application of a
biblical text than the mere drawing of a deduction: the
author had this to say: translated into our situation, that
would mean this. Effective preaching, we argued, contains,
as an essential ingredient, witness, witness to the truth of the
biblical message, but again it may well be possible to provide
my hearers with an opportunity to share their witness with
mine. A truth that they have discovered for themselves may
carry greater weight than a truth that I have told them.

We would also do well to recall again some of the
conclusions we reached in Chapter 2, viz. that meaning is
not exhausted by authorial intention; that while the author
should be given the first word, he should not be given the last
word; and that through being read in a new life-situation a
passage can shine in a new light and speak to our condition in
a way that the original author could never have envisaged.
Even if the ordained minister is in a privileged position for
discerning the original author's intention, the discernment
of this new illumination, the hearing of these new resonances, is not his or her peculiar privilege. Somehow, whether
in a study group held during the preceding week, as is Eduard
Schweizer's practice, or during the service itself, as I have
just suggested, or in some later gathering, called to reflect
together on what has been said, lay people must be given an
opportunity to speak of the things which they see and hear.

One advantage of bringing a group together after the
service is that it enables the preacher to hear how he or she
has been heard. I remarked in Chapter 2 that it is a source of

continual astonishment to some writers and speakers, particularly preachers, to discover how often they are perceived as saying something other than what they thought they were saying. For a preacher to hear how the sermon has, in fact, been heard, can be an illuminating as well as a salutary experience.

It should now be clear to the reader, particularly from the last chapter, that one of my aims in writing this book is to argue that preaching ought to continue to have a central place in our worship. I hope it will also be clear that I am not advocating one stereotyped method of preaching or a style of preaching which excludes all dialogue with the hearers. The active involvement of my hearers with the concerns of the text at certain clearly defined stages of our reflection upon it may well lead to a more effective engagement with the Word of God.

Telling the Story

There are other ways too in which new forms of preaching may well prove more effective than the sort of expository sermon with which we are familiar. Indeed, new forms would seem to be mandatory, in the light of conclusions we reached in Chapter 3. The conclusion which we reached in that chapter was that whereas argument has a clear tendency towards unambiguity, the force of an argument being weakened by any ambiguity, with narrative the opposite is true. Far from being weakened by ambiguity, its force is enriched by it.[39] We also reached the same conclusion about parables. Precisely because they too are stories or, alternatively, precisely because they are extended metaphors, they are too rich for their meaning to be reduced without remainder to a single sentence. However confident we may be that we have caught the main thrust of a parable, we are always left with the feeling that something of the parable's richness has been lost.[40]

We also saw that the differences between the letters, on the one hand, which are more argumentative in style, and the narratives and parables, on the other, are of more than merely literary significance but have a theological significance as well. For example, the fact that so much of the Bible consists of narrative tells us something about the faith to which it bears witness. We are dealing here with a faith which requires the speech form of narrative for its presentation.[41] Similarly, the fact that Jesus repeatedly has recourse to parable in order to speak about the kingdom of God tells us something about the nature of the kingdom itself.[42] Already in Chapter 3 I cited the conclusion drawn by Hans Weder that the interpreter of the parables must renounce the temptation to substitute for the parables some statement of theological principles derived from them. The interpreter should rather put the parable itself in the foreground and seek to enhance its force as a story by illuminating its structure and using paraphrase.[43] The same thing could be said about the interpretation of narrative proper. But if this is true of interpretation at the level of exegesis, it is surely no less true at the level of homiletical application. Instead of substituting for the parable or narrative some statement of theological principles hopefully derived from it, we preachers would do better to put the parable or narrative itself in the foreground and, after describing its probable historical setting, retell it in such a way that our hearers will hear it with enhanced force.

Let it be said at once, however, that this is no light task. The parable, in particular, is an extremely demanding literary form. A. M. Hunter has drawn attention to the paucity of effective parables in the literature of the world apart from the teaching of Jesus and has observed that it is difficult to name another person in history with more than one or two good ones to his credit.[44] Certainly anyone who has had the opportunity to read the Rabbinic parables collected by Fiebig will look in vain among them for the colour, the life, the teasing ambiguity that are hallmarks of the parables of Jesus.[45] Moreover, the parables of Jesus are remarkable for their verbal economy. Set any group of pastors or church people the task of transposing one of the parables of Jesus into a modern setting, and you will invariably find them producing stories of three or four times the length.

To illustrate the possibilities and problems of this method of exposition, I shall cite from the homiletical commentary on Luke by the Swiss scholar-preacher, Walter Lüthi, a part of his account of the story of the anointing of Jesus by a sinful woman in Luke 7.36–50.

This time it is a Pharisee who invites Jesus to a meal. Astonishing that an invitation should come from that quarter; equally astonishing that the Master accepts it. An act of hypocrisy? A trap? Yet in the course of the evening it will become clear that Simon was one of those few who had not reached a verdict about the rabbi from Nazareth prematurely but were still considering the question whether he was a prophet of God or not. In any case, people will have been agog on both sides to see how this meal worked out.

Right at the beginning Jesus has an experience which is not a favourable omen: he is received with a marked lack of courtesy. No bath of water for his feet, no attention to his hair, no customary kiss of welcome. In our stately homes there used to be two entrances, one for guests and one for servants, tradesmen and beggars. In the same way, Jesus had to enter the house of Simon the Pharisee, so to speak, by the side entrance.

And then comes the unexpected event, probably early in the evening. Anyone who invites the man from Nazareth can never be quite sure that everything will go according to plan, and is well advised to be prepared for surprises. An uninvited woman enters the room. How she managed to find her way in is a mystery. The doorkeeper can expect a reprimand later for this carelessness. And this woman is known to everyone as a prostitute, an object of public scandal. She is known to the host. How she plucked up courage to enter this house, in defiance of all good form and propriety, remains a mystery. Perhaps it was the courage of despair. She is looking for Jesus, the way people seek out a famous doctor to come and see some loved one who is dangerously ill. Until now she has not found the chance to meet him. This is an awkward situation, but she is dominated and driven by the one thought: this man, this one man, is able to rescue my wasted life.

And now she is standing there, looking around. She recognizes him, goes up to him and kneels at his feet. And then she breaks into audible weeping, smearing the floor and the feet of Jesus with her tears, and has nothing but her hair to wipe them away – how disgusting! And now she is kissing his feet – what extravagance! – and anointing his feet with ointment.

But, most astonishing of all, Jesus lets her do it. Such a theatre! such a scandal! And he does nothing and says nothing. The host has followed the scene carefully from the beginning. Surely Jesus knows this woman of the town? Surely he will civilly, but with all firmness, send her away? And, should she refuse, send her on her way with a kick? She should get the message then! But nothing of that happens. So the host concludes – no other possibility enters his head – that Jesus does not know the person he is dealing with. The question which till now he has left open is thereby answered: the man from Nazareth is no prophet. That the Master might know everything, that he might have a far deeper insight into the sinfulness and lostness of this pitiable woman, that he might want to help her and reach out his hand to her instead of giving her a kick, that he might even be able to forgive her sins and precisely in this way demonstrate his divine commission, that he has come to forgive sins and to rescue from death and hell – this possibility never enters his head.[46]

I have cited this passage as a good example of effective retelling of a biblical story, but note its length. All this and more by way of expansion of four verses of Luke. Nevertheless, the story does come across with enhanced force.

To Sum Up

This concludes our account of a basic pattern of exegesis and of a method of sermon preparation which follows on from it. At the beginning of the chapter I listed the essential exegetical steps. In the rest of the chapter we have been exploring one way of making the transition from exegesis to preaching. The essential steps in that process could be summarized as follows.

7. I ask myself, 'When have I or my people stood somewhere near to where the original readers of this passage

were standing and felt something like what they were feeling?'

8. I redirect the thrust intended by the original author so as to let it speak to my hearers. If a contemporary situation or spiritual state comparable to that addressed by the original author does not suggest itself, I concentrate my attention on the passage as a text rather than as a communication between this author and these readers. I also give more thought to the place of the passage within the Bible as a whole.

9. Having reflected upon the essential thrust of the passage both in its immediate context and in the wider context of the Bible, I ask myself, 'What is there that seems to speak against it? Do I, nevertheless, still believe it to be a word of importance for the lives of these people? If so, why?'

10. I consider the form of presentation. How shall I say what I now want above all to say? Can the literary form of the passage be reflected somehow in the sermon itself? How can I best catch and hold the attention of my hearers? Is there a way of engaging them in some sort of dialogue?

Too Much to Ask

If all this seems demanding, I can only reply that it cannot be otherwise. For my part, I have now been lecturing for twenty-two years and preaching off and on (sometimes more off than on) for thirty-eight but find preaching in some ways the harder thing to do. But if the claims we have made for preaching are justified, it stands under a peculiar promise.

The Mysterious Jar

I have long felt that a biblical story which contains a peculiarly apt image of the vocation of the preacher is the story of Elijah and the widow of Zarephath in I Kings 17. The widow's jar of flour and flask of oil seemed constantly on the point of giving out and yet were constantly and mysteriously renewed. So it is with preaching. Our resources too seem again and again to be on the point of giving out but again and again are mysteriously renewed. In the end, like Elijah and the widow of Zarephath, we too have nothing to rely on but a bare word, a word of promise and, on the face of it, an improbable one at that, but because we believe it is the promise of the living God, we may be of good heart.

An Ordination Sermon

Second Corinthians 12.9 – words of the risen Christ to the apostle Paul:

> It is enough for you to have my grace: it is in weakness that my power is fully felt.

The passage which was read tonight from II Corinthians 12 gives us a fascinating but tantalizingly brief insight into the inner life of the apostle Paul. He tells us, you'll remember, that there was given to him a thorn in the flesh, a messenger of Satan, to harass him. What exactly does he mean? We cannot be sure. It is quite likely, however, that he is referring to some form of sickness. Malaria? Maybe. A disease of the eyes? Epilepsy? Whatever it was, Paul begged the Lord three times over to take it way. And God didn't. It's not that Paul's prayer wasn't answered, but the answer he received was not the answer he was hoping for. This is what it was: 'It is enough for you to have my grace: it is in weakness that my power is fully felt.'

How does Paul feel about that answer now? In what sort of spirit does he recall it? In a spirit of resentment? Not at all. Rather in a spirit of deep gratitude. He can even go on to say this:

> Therefore I have cheerfully made up my mind to be proud of my weaknesses, because they mean a deeper experience of the power of Christ. I can even enjoy weaknesses, suffering, privations, persecutions and difficulties, for

Christ's sake. For my very weakness makes me strong in him.

All this may come as a bit of a shock to us, because the picture we have of the apostle Paul is likely to be a rather different one. That's not surprising, because there are two pictures of Paul to be found in the New Testament, the picture that emerges from Paul's own letters and the picture that we find in Acts. Our own image of Paul is likely to have been shaped more by Acts than by the letters, and that is a matter of some importance, because the pictures of Paul that are presented by these two sources are, in certain respects, strikingly different. The other lesson we heard tonight, from the Acts of the Apostles, brings out the difference very well.

It was the story of the visit of Paul and Barnabas to Lystra. At the end of that story Paul is actually stoned and for the moment thought to be dead. Yet it would be quite misleading to describe this story as a story of defeat. That's not the dominant note at all. Let's recall the details for a minute.

The story begins with Paul healing a cripple by his bare word of command. Electrified by this miracle, the crowds shout out, 'The gods have come down to us in human form!' Barnabas they call Zeus, and Paul they call Hermes, the messenger of the gods.

Paul and Barnabas check them with an eloquent appeal, but, even so, they barely prevent the crowd from offering sacrifice to them.

Then there's a sudden switch, and we read how Jews from other cities stirred up the crowd to stone Paul, and how he was dragged out of the city, thought to be dead. But that's not where the weight of the story falls. Luke devotes thirteen verses to the visit to Lystra, but the stoning of Paul takes up only one of them. And in the next verse Luke tells how Paul got to his feet, apparently unharmed, and went back into the city. The story as a whole doesn't leave the impression of weakness or defeat; it reads rather like a triumphal procession.

How does all this square up with Paul's own understanding of himself? If you only had Acts to go on, would you ever guess that Paul was a man who could write this:

'I came before you weak, nervous and shaking with fear'?

He does write that in his first letter to the Corinthians.

Or, again, would you ever guess, if you only had Acts to go on, that Paul had critics in the church who said of him, 'His letters are weighty and powerful, but when he appears he has no presence, and as a speaker he is beneath contempt'? He tells us about that in II Corinthians.

Or, again, would you ever guess, if you only had Acts to go on, that Paul could write words like these:

'It seems to me God has made us apostles the most abject of mankind. We are like men condemned to death in the arena, a spectacle to the whole universe – angels as well as men. . . We are treated as the scum of the earth, the dregs of humanity, to this very day'?

Or would you guess, if you only had Acts to go on, that Paul could write words like those we heard tonight:

'I have made up my mind to be proud of my weaknesses, because they mean a deeper experience of the power of Christ'?

There is, you see, quite a difference between the pictures of Paul presented by these two sources, Acts and Paul's own letters. One commentator on Acts, Ernst Haenchen, sums up the difference like this: 'Paul speaks of the power of Christ being shown forth in his weakness; what Luke describes is not the power of Christ in the weakness of Paul but the power of the Lord in the power of his disciple.' That puts it in a nutshell.

Here's how another writer puts it, the Swiss preacher, Walther Lüthi. Lüthi has written a little book about II Corinthians called *The Apostle*. In it he describes how a picture kept coming into his mind as he was writing the book, a picture from an old calendar which used to hang in his home as a child. It was a picture of a messenger – limping, with a wooden leg. The title? 'The Limping Messenger'. And Lüthi goes on:

The natural man prefers to picture a messenger the way the ancient Greeks pictured their god, Hermes, with wings

on both feet. It is the winged messenger, not the man with
the wooden leg, who corresponds to our wishful thinking.
But the messenger of Jesus is no winged Hermes. The
apostle Paul is more like that limping messenger.

Well, the Paul of Acts is more like a winged Hermes. In
fact, that's just what the people of Lystra took him to be –
Hermes in human form.

So we seem to have two Pauls, the Paul of Acts and the
Paul of the letters, the winged Hermes and the man with the
wooden leg. Which of them is the real Paul? Will the real Paul
please stand up?

I would not deny for a moment that Luke's picture has its
value but I have no doubt at all that Paul gives us a truer
picture of what it felt like at the time, what it felt like to be
there. Luke, after all, was not writing about himself but
about another man, whereas Paul was writing at first hand.
Luke, again, was writing after a considerable interval, thirty
years or thereabouts, whereas Paul's account is a report from
the thick of the fight. If we want to know what it really felt
like to be there, it is Paul to whom we must turn. If then we
let Paul be our guide rather than Luke, we will need to
recognize that it will be in our weakness rather than in our
strength that we too find the power of Christ in its fullness.

It would be very easy to state this point in a one-sided way.
The church wouldn't be ordaining you tonight at all if it
hadn't discerned in you gifts, gifts of nature enhanced by
grace, real strengths. And even in this passage Paul does not
say that it is *only* in weakness that Christ's power is felt.
What he does say, though, is that it is in weakness that that
power is *fully* felt, and it's that point that I want to dwell on
as something that is particularly relevant to all of us at those
times when we face tasks for which we seem to lack the
necessary gifts, times when we are conscious not of our
strength but of our weakness. I would like to point to two
areas in which I believe you will find this true. The first is
preaching.

Let me tell you of an experience I have had again and again,
and not only I myself – many other preachers I've known
have confessed to having it too. There are times when you

feel a certain satisfaction with the sermon you've just prepared for the following Sunday. You think you've made some telling points. You've introduced some apt illustrations. Sunday comes, and you deliver the sermon with conviction and enthusiasm. You go to the church door afterwards to shake hands with the congregation. Being human, you're half hoping someone will say a word of appreciation, and 'nobody says, "Boo".'

But there are also other times, times when you wrestle with a text and it seems to defeat you. Things don't fall into place, and you come down from the pulpit feeling that you are a most unworthy servant of the Word. And then, to your astonishment, someone gives your hand a grateful squeeze and thanks you for what you've said. Whenever this sort of thing happens, it shouldn't be seen as giving us an excuse for shoddy preparation next time, but it's a salutary experience. It brings home to us as nothing else can that if our Lord reaches men and women through our words he does it in spite of us as much as because of us. His power is shown forth not only in our strength but in our weakness.

Some of you will know the name of Leslie Tizard. He's probably best known as the author of a book called *Guide to Marriage*. But he was also a fine preacher and writer on preaching. In one of his books he talks about the times when we preachers have to drive ourselves up the pulpit steps and begin to wonder if God has withdrawn our commission. But, he goes on, I believe it often happens that when we are having most difficulty with ourselves we are most helpful to others. We are not always most convincing when our message comes easily and we can speak almost glibly. We may feel that we have had a good time, but few in our congregation may be the better for it. God may have used us much more effectively on a day when we have hardly known how to face our congregation, when it has been agony to preach at all, and we have come out of the pulpit with a sense of failure and a feeling that it would be a profound relief if we knew we should never have to preach again. For all our weakness, we have been used by the power of God.

Now for another area of ministry where again and again the same thing proves true, pastoral counselling. You've all of you, no doubt, been told that the first, second and third duty of any counsellor is to listen, to listen attentively and sympathetically. It sounds so easy. Surely anyone can listen? Surely this is a service which anyone is able to give? In fact, the opposite is true. Really to listen to an anxious person without cutting them short or jumping in prematurely with good advice – that is a very hard thing to do. It's especially hard for us ministers, because we like to think of ourselves as people who have the answers, people to whom other people come for advice.

Yes, listening is a difficult art. It can also be a disturbing experience. As you listen to another person talk over their problems, you may well become aware of painful echoes in your own mind. Then it may dawn on you that the very problem you're trying to help another person solve is your problem too, has been your problem for years, only you've pushed it out of your mind because you couldn't handle it.

That sort of discovery is a bitter pill for anyone to swallow, especially for a minister. There are two things you can do about it. On the one hand, you can shut your eyes and pretend that nothing has happened. But that way leads to a dead end, both for you and for your brother or sister. But there is also another way. You can step out of the role of professional superiority, admit that you are basically no different from your brother or sister and stand with him or her, waiting upon God for God's answer to you both. This may shatter your image of yourself as an omnicompetent pastor, but it is a royal road to the cross, a royal way to the knowledge of the crucified and risen Christ. Through the communion of weakness and sinfulness you will find the communion of saints. The power of Christ will be shown forth not in your strength but in your weakness, and you will enter still more deeply into the meaning of those words which Paul came to see as God's answer to his most anguished prayer, 'It is enough for you to have my grace: it is in weakness that my power is fully felt.'

We often don't want it to be that way. We would like to stride through the world like supermen or superwomen, equal to every occasion, adequate to meet every crisis, brushing aside every obstacle. We don't like being constantly driven to our knees and having to lift up empty hands to God.

Yet it is in weakness that God's power is fully felt. For it is only when we stretch out empty hands to God that he can fill them; only when we find that we are powerless that the way is open for his mighty power to be displayed; only when we see that we are as nothing that we see God truly, as the one who declares the guilty innocent, who gives life to the dead and calls to the things that are not that they be.

May it be your continual discovery that it *is* enough for you to have God's grace and that in your weakness his power *is* fully felt, as he gives to you, again and again, out of the immeasurable riches of his bounty.

Consider Him
Sermon on Hebrews 2.8 and 9

At present, we do not yet see everything subject to mankind; what our eyes do see is Jesus.

The letter to the Hebrews is possibly the least read of the longer books in the New Testament. And certainly there are parts of it which strike us nowadays as being very strange. All this detail about Old Testament sacrifices and the tabernacle in the wilderness, and all this talk of Christ as High Priest after the order of Melchizedek! Who was he, for goodness' sake?

Yet, for all its strangeness in parts, the letter to the Hebrews is a magnificent book and a most rewarding one to study; and in this passage the train of the author's thought is perfectly clear. He (or she) is talking about the destiny, the God-given task, of mankind, and to make his point – her point – the author quotes Psalm 8. According to Psalm 8, God has made mankind but little less than divine, and subjected all things to it. The author then underlines that 'all things' really means all things; there are no exceptions to this statement. In subjecting everything to mankind, God left nothing out. But, our author goes on, as yet this state of affairs is just not true. It is contrary to the evidence of our eyes. Mankind, men and women as we know them, fall short. They fall short of what they would *like* to be, of what they are *meant* to be. They have not yet attained that mastery of themselves and their world for which they were created. The whole of mankind represents an unfulfilled promise. But that is not the whole story. What our eyes do see is Jesus, and in him all our unfulfilled promise attains fulfilment.

There are many ways in which I could draw out what this author is saying, but I think the best way is to put it like this. There are some human qualities, qualities which command our admiration, which we instinctively think of as opposites. We instinctively think of them as opposites, because we find it extraordinarily difficult to hold them together. Where you find the one quality in a man or a woman, you don't often find the other. But these qualities, which we find so hard to hold together, are to be found united, in their fullness, in Jesus Christ.

Had I been preaching on this text twenty-five years ago, I might well have said that the one set of qualities is something you tend to find in men, and the other is something you tend to find in women. By now, I hope, I've begun to learn that the differences between men and women are more complicated than that. But the fact of the polarity of the qualities in question remains.

But what sort of qualities am I thinking of? I'm thinking, for example, of the qualities of courage and sensitivity. They are both admirable qualities, but you don't often find them together, at least in a marked degree. Some men and women do brave things, or things that are considered brave, simply because they haven't got the sensitivity to realize what danger they are in. They are, as we say, 'tough nuts'. Their insensitivity serves as a kind of screen between them and fear. There are other people who are acutely aware of all the realities of danger, of suffering and of death; indeed, their awareness is so acute that it proves too strong for them – in the hour of danger they are not able to bring themselves to do the brave thing. But these two qualities which we find so hard to hold together are found united, and in their fullness, in Jesus Christ.

Nothing is more evident in the Gospels than the courage of Jesus. When he set his face to go up to Jerusalem, and face almost certain death, that was an act of pure courage. He had to support him none of those props that make it easier for *us* to do brave things.

For example, it's easier to be brave when there's only one way left. But Jesus didn't have only one way left. When he went up to Jerusalem, it wasn't that he had no choice; he could have stayed away. No authority had summoned him to Jerusalem. No one would have fetched him to Jerusalem, had he not gone. His only reason for going was his conviction that this was his Father's will for him. Till the very last, he could have backed out. But he did not back out. He set his face steadfastly to go to Jerusalem when there were other much less frightful ways open to him.

And he did it without having any vestige of support from anyone else. It's ten times easier to be brave if you have others standing beside you. Jesus had no one who really stood beside him. There was no cheering, admiring crowd to urge him on. There wasn't a single soul in the world that understood why he had to go. There wasn't even an encouraging word from his friends. The only word he got from his friends was Peter's, telling him not to be so foolish and misguided. So he went alone.

It was, indeed, an act of pure courage, that long journey up to Jerusalem, but hand in hand with this courage, inseparably one with it, we see sensitivity. Every page of the Gospels is marked by the evidence of the extreme imaginative sensitivity of Jesus – to atmosphere, to the needs of others, to the inner reality of situations. And so his decision to go up to Jerusalem was not the act of your 'tough guy', whose courage is a sort of animal thing. It was the decision of one who saw only too well what lay in store for him and whose whole being shrank from it in apprehension. The story of Gethsemane makes clear what a heavy price he had to pay for his victory over his fears. There is a picture of Gethsemane in this very letter to the Hebrews, as graphic a picture of Gethsemane as any in the Bible.

'During the days of Jesus' life on earth', we read, 'he offered up prayers and petitions with loud cries and tears to the one who could save him from death.' Courage and sensitivity, present in their fullness, in the one person.

At present we do not yet see everything subject to mankind; what our eyes do see is Jesus.

What are some other admirable qualities which we find hard to hold together? How about authority and humility? Authority, the ability to lead, to challenge other people to rise to the heights of which they are capable — we admire that. But to combine authority with humility — that's the problem. Scratch a leader, and all too often you find a bully, someone with a need to manipulate, to dominate, other people. Let's look at the problem from the other side. Humility is without question a quality we admire. How it shines when it catches the light! But all too often what we call humility is something less than admirable. All too often it's mixed up with diffidence or with a self-disgust which in a strange twisted way is a kind of self-love.

But in Jesus what do we see? We see authority, to be sure, but we see authority that does not manipulate or dominate. He calls disciples to him with authority, and they obey him. Yet they remain free men and women, and they are able at any time to leave him, if they wish. We read in St John's Gospel that at one time many of his disciples did leave him, offended by his hard teaching. Then Jesus turns to the Twelve and asks them; 'Will you also go away?' It is a genuine question. 'If you wish to go, go; there is nothing to keep you.' Judas is even free to betray him, if he chooses.

But at the same time we see humility. Jesus rejects all fulsome compliments. To the woman in the crowd who calls out, 'Blessed is the mother who gave you birth and nursed you!' he replies, 'Blessed rather are those who hear the word of God and keep it!' And to the young man who runs up to him, falls on his knees before him and addresses him as 'Good Teacher', he answers, 'Why do you call me good? No one is good except God alone.' So we see authority and humility, present in their fullness, in the one person.

At present we do not yet see everything subject to mankind; what our eyes do see is Jesus.

And so we could go on. We could speak of him as the great example of the courteous rebel — a strange pair of words there! Courteous and yet a rebel, a gentle revolutionary. But the more we talk like this, the more insistently the question arises, 'So what?' What help is it to *us* to know that where *we* fail *he* succeeded? What use is he to us, this fully rounded man? If he is to be seen simply as an example, is he not an unattainable example? If he represents the ideal, is it not an impossible ideal?

Let us turn back to Hebrews. Who is Jesus Christ for the writer to the Hebrews? Example? Ideal? Yes, but much more than that. 'He is', says Hebrews, 'the author, as well as the finisher, of our faith.'

That word, usually translated 'author', is a highly significant word. 'Pioneer' or 'trail-blazer' might be a better translation. It's a word which is used of the founder of a city or a family or a philosophical school. One basic idea clings to the word through all these uses: an author or pioneer or founder begins something in order that others may enter into it. He founds a city, in order that others may some day live in it. He begins a family, so that some day others may be born into it. He founds a philosophical school, so that others may follow him into the truth. An author in this sense is one who blazes a trail for others to follow. This same understanding of Jesus Christ as trail-blazer underlies our text, the very text which contrasts our failure with his attainment.

Here too the author describes Jesus as pioneer, as the pioneer of our salvation; and it's also very important to notice just how he puts it in verses 8 and 9. The point is that he does not say, 'We do not see everything subject to mankind but we see Jesus', but rather, 'We do not *yet* see everything subject to mankind but we see Jesus.' He needs say no more than that everything is *not yet* subject to mankind – not yet, but it will be. What Jesus does, he does for us. What Jesus is, he is for us. As the Son of Man, he is the trail-blazer for all the sons and daughters of mankind. So what we see fulfilled in him is for us a sign of hope. As one writer puts it, 'Mankind's unfulfilled promise we see fulfilled in Christ, and for all mankind through Christ.'

And what must we do? Be honest with ourselves? Certainly. And yet in the end what's needed is not so much an act of self-examination as an act of self-commitment, a commitment of ourselves with all our problems of arrested growth and immaturity and unfulfilled promise to him, in trust and hope.

You could sum up the whole thrust of the letter to the Hebrews, in all its complexity and subtlety, in two short words, 'Consider him.' That's what the author's on about, again and again. 'Consider him, who is not ashamed to own us as his brethren.' 'Consider him, the pioneer and perfecter of our faith.' 'Consider him, so that you may not grow weary or fainthearted.' 'Consider him, for at present we do not yet see everything subject to mankind; what our eyes do see is Jesus.' Consider him, as you face whatever faces you now. Consider him, until you see nothing save Jesus only, and his grace will be with you through life and evermore.

A Sermon for Easter Day
Luke 24.5

'Why do you seek the living among the dead?'

When I look back on Easter sermons that I have heard in years gone by, as well as on Easter sermons that I have preached myself, I have the uneasy feeling that some of them have been long on affirmation and short on critical reflection.

'Christ is risen.' 'He is risen indeed.' But what do we really mean when we say that? How can we be sure that it's true? And what does his resurrection have to do with us?

So let's begin with some critical reflection on the story we heard read this morning from the Gospel of St Luke. Let's begin by asking, 'What is Luke really on about? What is he concerned to emphasize most of all?' We needn't fear that those questions will lead us somewhere remote from our own questions and concerns.

Luke tells us, you'll remember, of the visit of the women to the tomb, how they saw two angels, who told them that Jesus was risen, and how the women told all this to the apostles, who dismissed it as an idle tale.

Luke's story is based on an earlier account in Mark, but it's by no means a carbon copy. He's made some significant changes, which are a clue to the things he particularly wanted to emphasize, and these things stand out all the more clearly, when we read this story in the light of his Gospel as a whole. In choosing to emphasize the things that he does, he is addressing the questions of the readers he had in mind. I think we'll find that their questions are our questions too.

The first question he is addressing is, 'What is it all about? What do we mean when we say, "The Lord is risen"?' There's hardly any need to stress that that's a very important question – and a lively, contemporary question. You will remember the controversy that was triggered off a year or two ago by some pronouncement of the new Bishop of Durham.

Some writers nowadays would say that when we say, 'The Lord is risen', we are really talking about a divine act of vindication. It's all a way of saying that God has said 'Yes' to Jesus of Nazareth and all that he stood for; that he has rehabilitated him whom men rejected.

I don't think that there's any question that that's part of what the resurrection message is all about. We began our service this morning with a reading from Psalm 118. That psalm contains some words which are quoted again and again in the New Testament, because the first Christians saw them fulfilled in the resurrection of Jesus: 'The stone which the builders rejected has become the chief corner-stone.' Vindication, rehabilitation of the rejected one, reversal of the foolish judgment of men – that's certainly part of what the resurrection is all about.

Ask other modern writers what is the essence of the Easter faith for them, and they will say something like this: 'It's something which gives us grounds for hope. It's a sign, a promise of the new future which God has in store for all who believe in him, the new future that lies beyond death.'

Again, that's certainly part of it. There's no question of it. Listen again to the opening words of the reading we heard from I Peter: 'Blessed be the God and Father of our Lord Jesus Christ! By his great mercy we have been born anew to a living hope through the resurrection of Jesus Christ from the dead.' A sign of hope, the promise of a new future – again that's certainly part of what the resurrection is all about.

But I believe Luke would have said that, important as these things are, they are not as important, as central, as something else. He has left us in no doubt about what that something else is, where the heart of the matter lies for him. Listen again to the words of the angels to the women at the tomb, words peculiar to his Gospel: 'Why do you seek the living

among the dead?' Jesus as the living one, Jesus who is alive –
that is the heart of the Easter message for Luke. This is how
he summarizes the message of the angels later on in the
chapter. He tells how the women came back from the tomb
saying that they had seen a vision of angels, who said that he
was *alive*. And later on in his second volume, the book of
Acts, he tells how even the worldly, sceptical Festus, the
Roman governor of Judaea, got the point. Festus informs
King Agrippa that the dispute between Paul and the Jews all
had to do with one Jesus, who was dead, but whom Paul
asserted to be *alive*. That is where the heart of the matter lies
for Luke.

Fine, but dare we believe it? How can we be sure it's not a
lot of wishful thinking? an idle tale? That brings us to the
second question which I believe Luke is addressing through
this story. Luke is not only concerned to show his readers
what the resurrection message is all about; he is concerned to
show them that this is a message in which they can put their
trust.

Let's listen again to his account of the reactions of the
disciples to the report of the women who had been to the
tomb: 'These words seemed to them an idle tale, and they did
not believe them.' To the apostles it all appears to be so much
empty gossip. They have no trust in the news the women
bring. They don't even think it worth their while to go to the
tomb themselves to see if there might be something in the
story after all. What is Luke trying to get across to us in
telling us this? He's wanting to say that when those first
disciples came to believe that Jesus was risen, it wasn't
because they were in the mood to believe it. It wasn't because
the atmosphere about them was electric, charged with
expectation, so that any rumour spread like wildfire. No,
they were a thoroughly dispirited lot. Their reaction to the
story the women had to tell was to dismiss it as an idle tale, a
lot of hysterical talk. The bottom had dropped out of their
world, the sun had gone down, and their mood was one of
sombre despair.

The women themselves had some first glimmerings of
faith – at least, they reported what had happened to them at
the tomb – but they too were bewildered and perplexed. The

truth is – so Luke is telling us – that the disciples only came
to faith, even the women only came to full faith, because the
Lord himself overcame their despair and showed himself to
them to be alive.

'Ah,' you may say, 'that's great for them, but what about
us? For us to accept their message don't we have to make a
gigantic act of faith? Maybe they could claim, in all sincerity,
to have seen the Lord, but surely we can't.'

True, but neither could Luke's first readers. They too
belonged to a later generation than the generation of the first
eye-witnesses. They too, it seems, were asking essentially
the same questions that I was putting a moment ago: 'It was
fine for them, but what about us? How can we know that the
Lord is indeed alive?'

Luke is well aware that people of his own day are asking
that question, and he gives us a clear hint of his answer to it,
particularly in the next story, the story of the walk to
Emmaus. That story, like the others, is not just a story about
something that happened back there. It's meant to show each
generation of readers who Jesus is for them, for their day.
When Jesus draws near to the disciples, as they walk, and
joins them unrecognized, their hopes lie buried in the tomb
where they suppose he lies. The turning-point comes when
he responds to the downcast travellers by opening the
scriptures to them, so that their hearts burn within them.
The climax comes when they invite him to eat with them,
and he takes the bread, gives thanks, breaks it and gives it to
them. Luke is telling us how the eyes of those two disciples
were opened to recognize the risen Lord. But he is doing
more. He is showing his readers how any disciple of any age
or time may have their eyes opened to discern Christ's
presence. It is through word and sacrament: through the
preaching of the word and the sacrament of the broken bread.
To be sure, that is a veiled presence, a presence which is
grasped in faith, not something which can be demonstrated
for all to see, but nevertheless the real presence of the risen
Lord, who overcomes our despair, our unbelief.

So that's a second thing that Luke is seeking to get across
to us through this story. He is not only seeking to make clear
what resurrection is all about. He is telling us that this is a

message in which we can put our trust. The first disciples came to believe in it only because the Lord himself overcame their despair and showed himself to them to be alive. And that same Lord still makes his presence felt, though unseen, in the preaching of the word and the feast of the broken bread.

We can see already that the questions we want to raise about the resurrection were also vital ones for Luke and Luke's readers. But there's another question I raised at the beginning: 'What difference does it make? What difference does it make whether we believe it or not?' Luke is concerned with that question too, and through this story he's trying to point his readers to one of the many differences that the resurrection makes. He's trying to tell us that it throws light on the dark corners of our lives. I'm thinking now of the strong stress he makes, both in this story and in his other Easter stories, on the plan of God.

If you were to ask me to strip down my faith to its barest essentials and to state what I really believe in the fewest possible words, I might well say something like this: 'I believe God has a plan, a plan in which there is a place for me.' To be sure, it's not always easy for me to see it. There have been times when things happened to me that didn't seem to make any sense at all, but when I look back on them now I can begin to make some sense of them. I can see, for example, that through that painful experience back there I was being schooled to meet that crisis, years later. I recognize that someone else has had a hand in my life.

I think you probably know what I'm talking about. Pauline Webb once put it like this. 'There are the things,' she said, 'that take us by surprise but which later seem so often to be part of a design. There are the apparent coincidences that prove to have a significance for the subsequent course of our whole lives.' And then she went on to speak of a friend of hers who most of her life had been an agnostic but said towards the end of her days, not long before she died of cancer, that she began to believe that God was a real and living person, when she realized how in life's story he 'kept things up his sleeve'.

Well, Luke sees more clearly than the other evangelists that there is a pattern in the story he is telling. The story of Israel points forward to Jesus; and the story of Jesus leads inevitably to the church. God knows what he's up to; God knows where he's going. It all hangs together; it all makes sense.

At the centre of the story stands an event which seems to be the denial of all meaning in history, the cross. But the cross was not the end. It simply was not possible for Jesus to be held by death. Over and over again in his Easter stories Luke speaks of the cross and the resurrection of Jesus being part of the plan of God.

> The Son of Man had to be delivered into the hands of sinful men and be crucified and on the third day rise.

> Was it not necessary that the Christ should suffer these things and enter into his glory?

> Thus it is written that the Christ had to suffer and on the third day rise from the dead.

It had to be. It was all part of the plan. And therefore we can dare to believe that those things that happen to us that seem meaningless and pointless will also be seen one day to have had their place in God's plan for our lives, because the God in whom we put our trust is the one who transformed the judicial murder of Calvary into the triumph of Easter Day.

I made a rather slighting reference at the beginning to sermons which consist of nothing but affirmation. We've been working pretty hard this morning, and so perhaps we can permit ourselves too a moment of affirmation, a moment when we simply reflect about the meaning of this day and give thanks to God. Seven hundred years ago a medieval writer wrote a history of the Crusades. In it he described the capture of Jerusalem by the Crusaders and then went on to note that this happened in 1099, a year in which Urban II ruled as Bishop of Rome, Philip reigned in France, William Rufus reigned in England, and Jesus Christ was reigning for ever.

And to him with the Father and the Holy Spirit, the living, triune God, he ascribed, as is most justly due, all honour, power, might, majesty and dominion, henceforth and for evermore. Amen.

The Voice from the Cloud

A voice from the cloud said, 'This is my beloved Son, with whom I am well pleased; listen to him. . . .'
And when the disciples lifted up their eyes, they saw no one but Jesus only (Matt. 17.5,8).

We now see, far more clearly than we once did, that the books of the Bible were addressed, in the first place, not to no one in particular, but to specific circles of readers. They are not propositions, general truths, but communications, address. The different writings which make up the New Testament are not to be treated as chapters of a text book on Christian doctrine but as windows into living Christian communities.

New Testament scholars believe that the same thing holds good of the different units of which the Gospels are made up – the stories, the passages of teaching, the parables and the rest. These too were addressed, from the first, to specific circles of readers; indeed it was only because they were found to have something important to say to some group somewhere that they were preserved and transmitted at all.

So from the time this story of the Transfiguration first began to be told, it was told for a reason, it had a point. And it was told in such a way as to make that point most effectively. Everything irrelevant, everything that might blunt the point, has been dropped.

Another thing we now see more clearly than we once did is that the writers of the Bible use a great variety of literary forms, and that as the literary form of a passage varies so should the manner in which one handles it. Narrative, for example, is not the same thing as argument, and calls for a different sort of treatment.

In the oral tradition of camps and conferences there are some skits that are passed down from generation to generation. There is one such skit that I recall having seen many times. It is a parody of a sermon, a sermon on the text, 'Behold, Esau my brother is a hairy man, and I am a smooth man.' The preacher takes the text right out of its context and wrings every possible drop of meaning from it. The effect is hilarious. But why? What is it that makes it seem so utterly incongruous? Part of the answer, I suggest, is that a verse from a narrative is being handled as if it were a theologically loaded verse from a Pauline epistle. Compare it with a verse like this: 'I have been crucified with Christ: nevertheless I live; yet not I but Christ liveth in me.' There would be nothing incongruous about thinking that verse through step by step, but that's because it is a passage with an entirely different texture.

An appropriate image for a passage like that verse from Galatians would be that of a chain. The task of the interpreter is to establish, as clearly as possible, the way in which each statement advances the thought of the author, to scrutinize, if you like, each link in the chain. But with narrative you are dealing with something more like a series of pictures – or perhaps, better: a film, since the pictures are bound together into a unity by some pattern or movement running through them. So while no detail should be ignored, the primary focus of your attention should be the impact of the sequence as a whole, the overall pattern, the movement running through the whole.

So what about the story of the Transfiguration? Does it exhibit a pattern? Is there a movement running through it? I believe Willi Marxsen points us in the right direction when he speaks of a movement from transfiguration to the reality of everyday. At the end, the story, so to speak, strikes itself out. It is as if a curtain were drawn, and the disciples see nothing more, nothing but Jesus only, the Jesus whom they knew anyway, as they had long known him, no longer transfigured.

But that movement from transfiguration to the reality of everyday does not go unchallenged.

Master, it is well that we are here, let us make three
booths, one for you and one for Moses and one for Elijah.

What is Peter trying to do? I suggest that he is trying to
prolong a moment of insight.

The Gospels make it clear that the true identity of Jesus
was not self-evident to everyone. It could not be simply 'read
off' his person. Think of the different answers that we hear in
the Gospels to the question, 'Who is he?' There were those
who said, 'He is John the Baptist. He is Elijah. He is one of the
prophets.' But there were others who said, 'He is out of his
mind. He is the agent of Beelzebub. He is a blasphemer.'

And now what has happened? Peter has seen Jesus in a way
which shows him to belong to the world of God. He is the one
in whom the promises of God find fulfilment, the one to
whom Moses and Elijah, Law and Prophets, point. This is a
moment of insight, of certainty, and Peter is seeking to
prolong that moment. It is as if he were trying to forestall the
movement back to the reality of everyday with its uncertainty and ambiguity. This moment must not pass. It must
be held on to.

But it may not be. Peter did not know what he was saying.
'And when the disciples lifted their eyes, they saw no one but
Jesus only' – the Jesus who evoked unbelief as well as belief,
offence as well as acclaim. If this is a fair description of the
flow and counterflow of the story, what answer does it
suggest to the question, 'For whom was this story first told?'
It suggests that the story was first told for the benefit of
people who were seeking to prolong their moment of insight
and certainty, so that they might not have to live any longer
with uncertainty and ambiguity.

And what is the story saying to such people in a word? It is
saying that such moments cannot be prolonged. It is not
given to us to live all the time in a state of absolute certitude,
with the truths of the gospel for ever luminously self-
evident. Here we walk by faith, not by sight. Faith can
receive a strong impulse from moments when we see more
than usual, but we cannot perpetuate such moments inde-
finitely. And yet we have the voice which says, 'Listen to
him,' even when there is nothing more that is special to see.

That word seeks to accompany us from the cloud, from behind the curtain, the word that tells us that in this Jesus we have to do with God.

To most of us there are given from time to time truly mountain-top experiences, when all our doubts are swept away and we are simply overwhelmed by the reality of God in Christ. It may be at a camp or conference; it may be at some centre of pilgrimage like Taizé or Iona.

But then we go back home, to our own family and community and parish church, and what do we find? The relationships which were sour before we went away are sour still. The people who've been under the weather for years are battling still. It's all just too depressingly familiar. If only we could be back on the mountain top, at the camp site, at Taizé, on Iona! If only that sense of the immediate presence of God which we found there could carry on and never diminish! But it may not be.

And yet we still have his word, to which we cannot but listen, even if, for the moment, there seems to be nothing special to see, his word which claims not only an attentive ear but our hearts and minds and hands and feet. 'Listen to him.' That is God's word for us today, for today and tomorrow and the days that lie beyond.

That is a command, but a command that is rich with promise. For as we seek to put the words of Jesus into practice, our faith will be strengthened, not so dramatically as on the mountain top but no less surely. The knowledge that Jesus is indeed the way, the truth and the life only becomes our sure possession as we walk in his way and do his truth and live his life. It is to those who have the will to do God's will that it is given to know whether the word of Jesus is from God or whether it is of his own devising.

The heart of what I have been trying to say is summed up for us in this service of Holy Communion. Anything special to see? Hardly. A table, people, bread, wine. Nothing remarkable there. But at the heart of the service those lovingly preserved words of our Lord, words of command but, as surely, words of promise:

'Take. Eat. This is my body, which is for you. This cup is

the new covenant in my blood. Drink of it, all of you. For as often as you eat this bread and drink the cup, you proclaim the Lord's death, until he comes.'

Even so, come, Lord Jesus. Amen.

Notes

1. Introduction

1. Gordon D. Fee, *New Testament Exegesis: A Primer for Students and Pastors*, Westminster Press 1983, 25–50, 117–36.
2. Douglas K. Stuart, *Old Testament Exegesis: A Primer for Students and Pastors*, Westminster Press 1984, 23–43, 71–87.
3. Richard N. Soulen, *Handbook of Biblical Criticism*, John Knox Press, second ed. 1981, 235–39.

2. The Intention and the Words

1. For a discussion of the embarrassment which narrative caused to biblical scholars in the eighteenth and nineteenth centuries and of the different ways in which English-speaking and German-speaking scholars tried to deal with it see H. W. Frei, *The Eclipse of Biblical Narrative*, Yale University Press 1974. For a critical discussion of Frei's attempt to relate biblical narrative to prose realism see Stephen Prickett, *Words and the Word*, Cambridge University Press 1986, 76–78, 194f.
2. F. W. Beare, *The Earliest Records of Jesus*, Blackwell 1964, 238.
3. Eduard Schweizer, *The Good News According to Matthew*, SPCK 1976, 517.
4. Cf. O. Kaiser and W. G. Kümmel, *Exegetical Method*, Seabury Press 1967, 36; Willi Marxsen, *Introduction to the New Testament*, Blackwell 1970, 10; R. H. Fuller, *The Use of the Bible in Preaching*, Bible Reading Fellowship 1981, 41.
5. Cf. W. G. Kümmel, *The New Testament: The History of the Investigation of its Problems*, SCM Press 1963, 62–69, 98–104.
6. Karl Barth, *The Epistle to the Romans*, translated from the sixth edition by E. C. Hoskyns; Oxford University Press 1933, 6.
7. Barth, *Romans*, 8.
8. Ibid., 7f.
9. John Barton, *Reading the Old Testament*, Darton, Longman & Todd 1984, 181.

10. Ibid., 182.

11. Cf. Frank Lentricchia, *After the New Criticism*, University of Chicago Press 1980.

12. Brevard S. Childs, *The New Testament as Canon: An Introduction*, SCM Press 1984, 35f., 45. For full discussions of Childs' writings prior to *The NT as Canon* see especially James Barr, *Holy Scripture: Canon, Authority, Criticism*, Clarendon Press 1983, 130–71; Barton, *Reading the OT*, 77–103, 140–57.

13. Ulrich Luz, 'Erwägungen zur sachgemässen Interpretation neutestamentlicher Texte', *Evangelische Theologie*, 42 (1982), 493–518; cf. Ernesto Cardenal, *Das Evangelium der Bauern von Solentiname*, Gerd Mohn 1979.

14. Walter Wink, *Transforming Bible Study*, SCM Press 1981, 17f.

15. W. K. Wimsatt and Monroe C. Beardsley, 'The Intentional Fallacy', *Sewanee Review*, LIV (1946), 468–88; reprinted in David Newton-De Molina (ed.), *On Literary Intention*, Edinburgh University Press 1976, 1–13.

16. M. C. Beardsley and W. K. Wimsatt, 'Intention', in Joseph T. Shipley (ed.), *Dictionary of World Literature*, Routledge 1945, 326–29.

17. W. K. Wimsatt, 'Genesis: A Fallacy Revisited' in Newton-De Molina, *On Literary Intention*, 136; cf. 116, 128.

18. Wimsatt and Beardsley, 'Intention', 326, 327, 328.

19. Cf. Theodore Redpath, 'The Meaning of a Poem', in Newton-De Molina, *On Literary Intention*, 20.

20. E. D. Hirsch Jr., 'Three Dimensions of Hermeneutics', in Newton-De Molina, *On Literary Intention*, 196, 207f.

21. Ibid., 207.

22. Anthony C. Thiselton, 'Reader-Response Hermeneutics, Action Models and the Parables of Jesus', in Lundin/Thiselton/Walhout, *The Responsibility of Hermeneutics*, Eerdmans/Paternoster 1985, 107–13.

23. See A. Deissmann, *Light from the Ancient East*, Hodder & Stoughton 1910, 228–39. To show that people were aware of this distinction even in the early centuries of the church, Deissmann cites a reference by Eusebius to the writings of Dionysius of Alexandria as containing 'both letters and copious treatises written in the manner of letters' (see 229 note 2).

24. Barton, *Reading the OT*, 114, cf. 105.

25. For further accounts of form criticism and redaction criticism as applied both to the Old Testament and the New see Barton, *Reading the OT*, 30–60; Stephen Neill, *The Interpretation of the New Testament 1861–1961*, Oxford University Press 1964, 236–91.

26. Austin Farrer, *A Study in St Mark*, A. & C. Black 1951, 7f.

27. Cf. David Hill, 'Prophecy and Prophets in The Revelation of

St. John', *NTS*, 18 (1971–72), 401–18. Klaus Koch has argued cogently that Daniel also was originally regarded as a prophetic book and was later, possibly after the Jewish revolts, transferred by the influential rabbis to the Writings. See his article, 'Is Daniel also among the Prophets?' *Interpretation*, 39 (1985), 117–30.

28. See K. P. Donfried (ed.), *The Romans Debate*, Augsburg 1977, for various discussions of the problem.

29. For a full discussion see R. Maddox, *The Purpose of Luke Acts*, Vandenhoeck & Ruprecht and T. & T. Clark 1982.

30. Barton, *Reading the OT*, 58.

31. Cf. Ernest Best, *Mark: The Gospel as Story*, T. & T. Clark 1983, 9–15. Morna D. Hooker, *The Message of Mark*, Epworth 1983, 21–24.

32. C. K. Barrett, *Luke the Historian in Recent Study*, Epworth 1961, 63.

33. See e.g. Martin Kiddle, *The Revelation of St John*, Hodder & Stoughton 1940, 144; Robert H. Mounce, *The Book of Revelation*, Eerdmanns 1977, 178f.

34. M. Rissi, *Time and History*, John Knox 1966, 4–6.

35. See R. H. Charles, *A Critical and Exegetical Commentary on the Revelation of St John*, T. & T. Clark 1920, 223f; G. B. Caird, *A Commentary on the Revelation of St John the Divine*, A. & C. Black 1966, 106f; G. R. Beasley-Murray, *The Book of Revelation*, Oliphants 1974, 149f.

36. Cf. James D. G. Dunn, 'Levels of Canonical Authority', *Horizons in Biblical Theology*, 4 (1982), 43.

37. Cf. Gerd Theissen, *The Social Setting of Pauline Christianity*, T. & T. Clark 1982; Bruce J. Malina, *The New Testament World: Insights from Cultural Anthropology*, SCM Press 1983; Derek Tidball, *An Introduction to the Sociology of the New Testament*, Paternoster 1983; A. J. Malherbe, *Social Aspects of Early Christianity*, Fortress Press 1983.

38. Wimsatt, 'Genesis', 136.

39. F. R. Leavis, 'Literary Criticism and Philosophy: A Reply', *Scrutiny*, 6 (1937), 61.

40. Cf. Gerhard Ebeling, 'Church History is the History of the Exposition of Scripture', *The Word of God and Tradition*, Collins 1968, 28.

41. Ulrich Luz, *Das Evangelium nach Matthäus*, Benziger/Neukirchener Verlag 1985, 1, 79.

42. For a full discussion of ways in which our culture differs from the cultures reflected in the Bible see Ernest Best, *From Text to Sermon*, St Andrew Press 1978, ch. 2.

43. Luz, *Evangelium nach Matthäus*, 80.

44. Victor Gollancz, *My Dear Timothy*, Gollancz 1952, 48, 88–94.

45. Corrie ten Boom, *The Hiding Place*, Hodder & Stoughton 1972, 182.

46. Hans-Georg Gadamer, *Truth and Method*, Sheed & Ward 1979, 264f.

47. Cf. Gerhard Ebeling, *The Truth of the Gospel*, SCM Press 1985, 23.

48. Nigel M. Watson, '"To make us rely not on ourselves but on God who raises the dead" – 2 Cor. 1, 9b as the Heart of Paul's Theology', in U. Luz and H. Weder (eds.), *Die Mitte des Neuen Testaments: Festschrift für Eduard Schweizer*, Vandenhoeck & Ruprecht 1983, 384–98.

49. According to Liddell and Scott, the word *exēgēsis* carries the meanings of 'statement', 'narrative' or 'explanation', 'interpretation', but in a general sense, e.g. of laws or dreams.

50. See e.g. the analysis by Stephen Prickett of the poem by G. M. Hopkins, 'As kingfishers catch fire', in *Words and the Word* 119–23. Prickett takes up the words, 'Christ plays in ten thousand places', and finds in them no fewer than seven levels of meaning.

51. Plato, *Apology*, 22b–c.

52. For a full discussion of the different ways in which the inspiration of the Bible has been understood in different traditions see W. J. Abraham, *The Divine Inspiration of Holy Scripture*, Oxford University Press 1981.

53. So, e.g., Barton, *Reading the OT*, 175f.

54. Cf. E. D. Hirsch, 'Objective Interpretation' in Newton-De Molina, *On Literary Intention* (first published in 1960), 27.

55. See e.g. A. J. Close, 'Don Quixote and the "Intentionalist Fallacy"' in Newton-De Molina, *On Literary Intention*, 189; George Watson, 'The Literary Past', *On Literary Intention*, 167.

56. As an illustration of subconscious motivation George Watson cites Matthew Arnold's poem, 'Sohrab and Rustum', in which a strong son is slain by a mightier father. It does not seem at all fanciful to find in this poem an expression of the poet's subconscious resentment against his own father, a famous headmaster. See George Watson, 'The Literary Past', in Newton-De Molina, *On Literary Intention*, 168f.

57. Graham Hough, 'An Eighth Type of Ambiguity', *On Literary Intention*, 232.

58. See A. Feuillet, 'La Dignité et le Rôle de la Femme', *NTS*, 21 (1975), 159–62.

59. For fuller accounts see Hannelore Link, *Rezeptionsforschung*, Kohlammer 1976; Wolfgang Iser, *The Act of Reading*, Routledge & Kegan Paul 1978.

60. Cf. Hans Conzelmann, *I Corinthians*, Fortress Press 1975, 246.

61. For a critical discussion of Childs' book, *The New Testament*

as *Canon*, see my review in *Austr. Bib. Rev.*, 36 (1986), 72f.

62. Cf. R. H. Stein, *An Introduction to the Parables of Jesus*, Westminster Press and Paternoster 1981, 42–52.

63. Birger Gerhardsson has argued that a case can be made for a modified form of the allegorical interpretation as representing the intention of Jesus himself. According to him, the question which the parable dealt with originally was, 'Who is the true shepherd of the people of God?' In its present setting, however, the parable clearly has to do not with shepherds but with neighbours. See Birger Gerhardsson, *The Good Samaritan – The Good Shepherd?*, Coniectanea Neo-Testamentica XVI, Gleerup 1958.

64. Hans Weder, *Die Gleichnisse Jesu als Metaphern*, Vandenhoeck & Ruprecht 1978, 95.

65. Dunn, 'Levels of Canonical Authority', 26. The distinction made here is presupposed in the final chapter in relation to Step 9 of the recommended procedure for sermon preparation.

66. Cf. Erich Dinkler, *'Bibelkritik II'*, in Kurt Galling et al. (eds), *RGG* third ed., J. C. B. Mohr 1957, I, 1190.

67. Schweizer, *Matthew*, 518–21.

68. Ibid., 520; cf. 525–27.

69. Ibid., 521 (my own translation).

70. Gadamer, *Truth and Method*, 264f.

71. See U. Luz *'Erwägungen . . .'*, 504f; also *'Vom Sinn biblischer Texte'*, in Georg Pöhlmann (ed.), *Worin besteht der Sinn des Lebens?*, Gerd Mohn 1985, 86.

3. The Typical and the Unique: the Importance of Genre

1. Frank Kermode, *The Genesis of Secrecy: On the Interpretation of Narrative*, Harvard University Press 1979, 162f.

2. John Barton, *Reading the Old Testament: Method in Biblical Study*, Darton, Longman & Todd 1984, 17.

3. C. S. Lewis, for example, speaking of the origin of his Narnia books, writes that 'everything began with images: a faun carrying an umbrella, a queen on a sledge, a magnificent lion' (*Of This and Other Worlds*, Collins 1982, 72).

4. For the background to Galatians see especially C. K. Barrett, *Freedom and Obligation: A Study of the Epistle to the Galatians*, SPCK 1985. On p. 18 Barrett stresses the importance for the understanding of Galatians of noting that Paul is *arguing* and that just beneath the surface of what he says one may easily find the thought, and often the language, of his opponents.

5. Cf. C. K. Barrett, *A Commentary on the Second Epistle to the Corinthians*, A. & C. Black 1973, 28–30; also 'Paul's Opponents in II Corinthians', *NTS*, XVII (1971), 233–54.

6. Cf. C. K. Barrett, *A Commentary on the First Epistle to the Corinthians*, A. & C. Black 1968, 109; James D. G. Dunn, *Unity*

and Diversity in the New Testament, SCM Press 1977, 275–79.

7. Hans Weder, 'Zum Problem einer christlichen Exegese', *NTS*, 27 (1980/81), 69–71.

8. For example, the study by Warren S. Kissinger, *The Parables of Jesus: A History of Interpretation and Bibliography*, Scarecrow and ATLA 1979, combines more than 200 pages of text on the history of the interpretation of the parables with an equally lengthy section of bibliography.

9. Joachim Jeremias, *The Parables of Jesus*, SCM Press 1954, 19.

10. Pierre Grelot, 'Le père et ses deux fils: Luc XV, 11–32,' *RB*, 84 (1977), 326–47.

11. Sallie McFague, *Speaking in Parables*, SCM Press 1976, 49.

12. Ibid., 39.

13. Ibid., 5, 40.

14. Hans Weder, *Die Gleichnisse Jesu als Metaphern*, Vandenhoeck & Ruprecht 1978, 90.

15. Douglas Berggren, 'The Use and Abuse of Metaphor', *Review of Metaphysics*, December 1962, 243f.

16. Weder, *Gleichnisse Jesu*, 90.

17. McFague, *Speaking in Parables*, 69.

18. Ibid., 15.

19. C. H. Dodd, *The Parables of the Kingdom*, Nisbet 1935, 16.

20. Jeremias, op. cit., p. 88 sets out seven laws of transformation to which the parables have been subject. For a good short account of this process of transformation see T. W. Manson, *Ethics and the Gospel*, SCM Press 1960, 93–103.

21. Jeremias, op. cit., 88.

22. For a further account of these distinctions see E. Linnemann, *Parables of Jesus*, SPCK 1966, 3–8.

23. McFague, *Speaking in Parables*, 122.

24. Ibid., 78.

25. For a full discussion see Klyne Snodgrass, *The Parable of the Wicked Tenants*, J. C. B. Mohr 1983.

26. Quoted by McFague, *Speaking in Parables*, 76.

27. See Jeremias, op. cit., 22.

28. McFague, *Speaking in Parables*, 3 (cf. 37).

29. For an elaboration of this distinction see G. A. Deissmann, *Light from the Ancient East*, 228–45.

30. Günther Bornkamm, *Paul*, Hodder & Stoughton 1971, XXV.

31. Cf. Nigel M. Watson, 'Willi Marxsen's Approach to Christology', *ExpT*, 97 (1985), 41f.

32. Rowan Williams, *Resurrection*, Darton, Longman & Todd 1982, 96.

33. C. H. Dodd, *The Interpretation of the Fourth Gospel*, CUP 1953, 383. For an excellent example of sensitivity to the differences in colour and texture between two passages from the Gospels

which exhibit the same literary form see Graeme Griffin, 'The colour of joy', in Nigel Watson (ed.), *Jesus Christ for Us*, Melbourne: Joint Board of Christian Education 1982, 55–60.

34. C. H. Dodd, *The Epistle of Paul to the Romans*, Hodder & Stoughton 1932, 133.

35. David Daiches, *A Study of Literature for Readers and Critics*, André Deutsch 1968, 9.

36. See John Barton, *Reading the OT* (11–16, 134–35), for a discussion of the usefulness of this expression. Barton himself defines it principally as the ability to recognize genre.

4. The Whole and the Parts

1. Willi Marxsen, *Der erste Brief an die Thessalonicher*, Theologischer Verlag 1979, 10.

2. Max-Alain Chevallier, *L'Exégèse du nouveau Testament*, Labor et Fides 1985, 87.

3. Chevallier, *L'Exégèse*, 92.

4. Ibid., 83.

5. See Lewis S. Mudge, 'Hermeneutical Circle', in Alan Richardson and John Bowden (eds), *A New Dictionary of Christian Theology*, SCM Press 1983, 249f.

6. Marxsen, *I Thessalonicher*, 10.

7. Gadamer, *Truth and Method*, 236.

8. Ibid., 261.

9. Ibid., 238.

10. Cf. Chevallier, *L'Exégèse*, 85–87.

11. Maddox, *The Purpose of Luke–Acts*, 186f.

12. See above, pp. 26, 28.

13. Cf. Maddox, *The Purpose of Luke – Acts*, 182–87.

14. E.-B. Allo, *Saint Paul: Seconde Épître aux Corinthiens*, Gabalda 1956, 121, 153.

15. G. Didier, *Désintéressement du Chrétien*, Aubier 1955, 107.

5. Past and Present

1. Cf. Leander E. Keck, *The Bible in the Pulpit*, Abingdon 1978, 110.

2. See above pp. 72ff.

3. J. A. Ziesler, *The Meaning of Righteousness in Paul*, Cambridge University Press 1972, 210.

4. See F. Hahn, 'Taufe und Rechtfertigung', G. Strecker, 'Befreiung und Rechtfertigung', in J. Friedrich *et al.* (eds), *Rechtfertigung*, Mohr/Vandenhoeck & Ruprecht 1976, 112–15, 501–3.

5. R. A. Knox, *On Englishing the Bible*, Sheed & Ward 1949, 10.

6. Ferdinand de Saussure, *Course in General Linguistics*, Collins 1974, 88f.

7. Knox, *On Englishing the Bible*, 10f.

188 *Striking Home*

8. Cf. C. H. Dodd, 'Some Problems of New Testament Translation', *ExpT*, 72 (1960–61), 271.

9. Eugene van Ness Goetchius, *The Language of the New Testament*, Scribners 1967, 18f.

10. *On Englishing the Bible*, 11.

11. Cf. James Barr, 'Common Sense and Biblical Language', a review of David Hill, *Greek Words and Hebrew Meanings*, Cambridge University Press 1967, *Biblica*, 49 (1968), 381.

12. Sophocles, *Philoctetes*, 781; *Pap. Ryl.*, 119:14.

13. Plato, *Laws*, 934b. For full discussions of the linguistic evidence see E. de W. Burton, *The Epistle to the Galatians*, T. & T. Clark 1921, 463 ff.; C. H. Dodd, *The Bible and the Greeks*, Hodder & Stoughton 1954, 5off.; Ziesler, *Meaning of Righteousness*, 19f.

14. G. B. Caird, *The Language and Imagery of the Bible*, Duckworth 1980, 77f.

15. Amos 2.6f.; 5.17; Micah 3.9–11; cf. Ps. 27.12; 35.11; Prov. 6.19; 12.17; Dan. 13.28f.

16. Cf. E. Schweizer, *Jesus*, SCM Press 1968, 99.

17. Cf. W. D. Davies, *Invitation to the New Testament*, Doubleday 1966, 39–49.

18. James Barr, *The Semantics of Biblical Language*, Oxford University Press 1961, 100–6, 114–16, 133–40. For a valuable discussion of the issues raised by Barr see Norman W. Porteous, 'Second Thoughts: The Present State of Old Testament Theology', *ExpT*, 75 (1963–64), 70–74.

19. Gadamer, *Truth and Method*, 237.

20. Barr, *Semantics*, 263.

21. Th. C. Vriezen, *Die Erwählung Israels nach dem Alten Testament*, Zwingli 1953; also *An Outline of Old Testament Theology*, Blackwell, second ed., 1970, 315f.

22. *The Good News Bible*, The Bible Societies 1976, VIII.

23. Prickett, *Words and the Word*, 10.

24. Ibid., 224.

25. Ibid., 162.

26. Ibid., 224.

27. Ibid., 242.

28. Ibid., 11.

29. Ibid., 7.

30. Ibid., 153.

31. Ibid., 222f.

32. Ibid., 155f.; cf. 223.

33. Ibid., 166.

34. Ibid., 224.

35. Ibid., 32.

36. T. W. Manson, *On Paul and John*, SCM Press 1963, 63.

37. Barn. 4.10, 13; 15.7.

38. Origen, *Hom.* 2.4, *On Lev.* 2.4.
39. Campbell N. Moody, *The Mind of the Early Converts*, Hodder & Stoughton 1920, 246.

6. *Why Preach?*

1. Gerhard Ebeling, *The Nature of Christian Faith*, Collins 1961, 15.
2. Cited by Martin Kriener, *Aporien der politischen Predigt*, Kaiser 1974, 8, note 5.
3. Cf. Yngve Brilioth, *A Brief History of Preaching*, Fortress Press 1965 (Swedish original: Gleerup 1945), 11f., 26f.
4. C. H. Dodd, *The Apostolic Preaching and its Developments*, Hodder & Stoughton 1936, 4.
5. Cf. Joachim Jeremias, *The Sermon on the Mount*, Athlone Press 1961, 21.
6. Cf. Jeremias, *Sermon on the Mount*, 21f.; cf. also what was said in Chapter 3 about the adaptation of the parables so as to speak to the new situation of the church at a later time. See above, pp. 72–74.
7. Cf. Eduard Schweizer, *The Lord's Supper*, Fortress Press 1967, 35f.
8. Chrysostom, *Homilies on Romans* on Rom 1.16.
9. Cf. Blass/Debrunner/Rehkopf, *Grammatik des neutestamentlichen Griechisch*, fourteenth ed., Vandenhoeck & Ruprecht 1976, 354, n.3.
10. Rudolf Bultmann, 'Jesus und Paulus', *Exegetica*, J. C. B. Mohr 1967 (German original: 1936), 227f. (my own translation).
11. Cf. the three elements identified by Brilioth as basic to the sermon of Jesus in the synagogue at Nazareth, viz. the liturgical, the exegetical and the prophetic. He also argues that these three elements have profoundly influenced the subsequent development of Christian preaching. (*A Brief History of Preaching*, 8–11.)
12. Bernard Lord Manning, *A Layman in the Ministry*, The Independent Press 1942, 145. Cf. H. H. Farmer, *The Servant of the Word*, Nisbet 1941, 93: 'Preaching is essentially a pastoral activity. It is part of a pastoral relationship, one activity of a settled and continuous ministry.'

7. *From Exegete to Preacher*

1. Cf. above, ch. 4, pp. 83–87.
2. Cf. Ch. 2, 30f. Ch. 5, pp. 89–95.
3. Cf. Ch. 3, pp. 50–76.
4. Cf. Ch. 3, pp. 76–82.
5. Cf. Ch. 4, p. 87.
6. Cf. Ch. 5, pp. 106f.
7. Cf. Ch. 5, pp. 96–99.

8. Cf. Ch. 5, pp. 99–106.

9. Cf. Ch. 4, p. 87.

10. Cf. Ch. 2, pp. 5–11.

11. Cf. Ch. 2, pp. 35–48.

12. *The Integrity of Preaching*, 15–23.

13. Archibald Alexander, *The Stuff of Life*, Allenson, no date, 231.

14. *The Integrity of Preaching*, 15–23.

15. Willi Marxsen, 'Der Beitrag der wissenschaftlichen Exegese des Neuen Testaments für die Verkündigung', *Der Exeget als Theologe*, Gerd Mohn 1968, 69.

16. Leander E. Keck, *The Bible in the Pulpit*, Abingdon 1978, 82.

17. Scc above, p. 8.

18. See above, pp. 90f.; cf. 26, 28.

19. See above, pp. 85–87.

20. See above, pp. 22f.

21. See above, pp. 28f.

22. C. F. D. Moule, *The Birth of the New Testament*, A. & C. Black 1962, 92.

23. Nicholas Lash, 'What Might Martyrdom Mean?' *Theology on the Way to Emmaus*, SCM Prcss 1986, 80f.

24. H. H. Farmer, *The Servant of the Word*, Nisbet 1941, 107; cf. Detlev Dormeyer, *Die Bibel antwortet*, Pfeiffer/Vandenhoeck 1978, 38f.

25. Ernest Best, *From Text to Sermon*, St Andrew Press 1978, 33–36.

26. Best, *From Text to Sermon*, 32f.

27. *The Epistle to the Romans*, 7; cf. Keck *The Bible in the Pulpit*, 117: 'The continuities between today's church and that of the New Testament . . . are a given, because certain perversions of life and Christian faith are perennial, paradigmatic, indeed, one may even call them archetypal.'

28. David Daiches, *God and the Poets*, Clarendon Press 1984, 219.

29. Dietrich Bonhoeffer, *The Cost of Discipleship*, SCM Press 1959, 44f.

30. Cf. Nigel M. Watson, 'To make us rely . . .', 384–98.

31. Best, *From Text to Sermon*, 73f.

32. Eduard Schweizer, *Gott Will zu Worte Kommen*, Kaiser 1978, 9–12.

33. Ulrich Luz maintains that, quite apart from preaching, the true understanding of biblical texts is the task of the whole person and calls for engagement, commitment, venture and suffering. See *Das Evangelium nach Matthäus*, 81.

34. Cf. R. E. C. Browne, *The Ministry of the Word*, SCM Press 1958, 20.

35. John Baillie, *Invitation to Pilgrimage*, Oxford University Press 1942, 25.

36. Keck, *The Bible in the Pulpit*, 47; cf. what he says on pp. 63–66 about the value of the sermon saying out loud what we do not like to hear in the text; that is, of the preacher anticipating openly, and as trenchantly as possible, the anticipated (and known) responses of the congregation to the text and its theme.

37. Chevallier, *L'Exégèse du nouveau Testament*, 81.

38. A. M. Hadfield, *An Introduction to Charles Williams*, Robert Hale 1959, 96–98.

39. Cf. above, pp. 60–63.

40. Cf. above, pp. 67–74.

41. Cf. above, p. 65.

42. Cf. above, p. 71.

43. Cf. above, pp. 71f.

44. A. M. Hunter, *The Parables Then and Now*, SCM Press 1971, 15.

45. I am here dependent on class notes studied under Joachim Jeremias at Göttingen thirty years ago.

46. Walter Lüthi, *Das Lukasevangelium, ausgelegt für die Gemeinde*, Friedrich Reinhardt, no date 248–50 (my own translation). For excellent examples of preaching in which the literary form of the biblical passage is reflected in the sermon itself see Frederick Buechner, *Telling the Truth: The Gospel as Tragedy, Comedy and Fairy Tale*, Harper & Row 1977; Don. M. Wardlaw (ed.), *Preaching Biblically*, Westminster Press 1983. For a forceful argument to the effect that arriving at something to say and determining how to say it are two distinct processes see Fred B. Craddock, *Preaching*, Abingdon 1985, 84f.

Bibliography

Abraham, W. J., *The Divine Inspiration of Holy Scripture*, Oxford: OUP 1981.

Alexander, Archibald, *The Stuff of Life*, London: Allenson, no date.

Allo, E. B., *Saint Paul: Seconde Épître aux Corinthiens*, Paris: Gabalda 1956.

Baillie, John, *Invitation to Pilgrimage*, Oxford: OUP 1942.

Barr, James, 'Common Sense and Biblical Language', *Biblica*, 49 (1968), 377–87.

——, *Holy Scripture: Canon, Authority, Criticism*, Oxford: Clarendon Press 1983.

——, *The Semantics of Biblical Language*, Oxford: OUP 1961.

Barrett, C. K., *A Commentary on the First Epistle to the Corinthians*, London: A. & C. Black 1968.

——, *A Commentary on the Second Epistle to the Corinthians*, London: A. & C. Black 1973.

——, *Freedom and Obligation: A Study of the Epistle to the Galatians*, London: SPCK 1985.

——, *Luke the Historian in Recent Study*, London: Epworth 1961.

Barth, Karl, *The Epistle to the Romans*, translated from the sixth edition by E. C. Hoskyns; London: OUP 1933.

Barton, John, *Reading the Old Testament*, London: DLT 1984.

Beardsley, M. C. and Wimsatt, W. K., 'Intention', in Joseph T. Shipley (ed.), *Dictionary of World Literature*, London: Routledge 1945 326–29.

Beare, F. W., *The Earliest Records of Jesus*, Oxford: Basil Blackwell 1964.

Beasley-Murray, G. R., *The Book of Revelation*, London: Oliphants 1974.

Berggren, Douglas, 'The Use and Abuse of Metaphor', *Review of Metaphysics*, 16 (1962–63), 237–58, 450–72.

Best, Ernest, *From Text to Sermon*, Edinburgh: St Andrew Press 1978.

——, *Mark: The Gospel as Story*, Edinburgh: T. & T. Clark 1983.

194   *Striking Home*

Blass/Debrunner/Rehkopf, *Grammatik des neutestamentlichen Griechisch*, fourteenth ed: Göttingen: Vandenhoeck & Ruprecht 1976.

Bonhoeffer, Dietrich, *The Cost of Discipleship*, London: SCM Press 1959.

Bornkamm, Günther, *Paul*, London: Hodder & Stoughton 1971.

Brilioth, Yngve, *A Brief History of Preaching*, Philadelphia: Fortress Press 1965.

Browne, R. E. C., *The Ministry of the Word*, London: SCM Press 1958.

Buechner, Frederick, *Telling the Truth: The Gospel as Tragedy, Comedy and Fairy Tale*, New York: Harper & Row 1977.

Bultmann, Rudolf, 'Jesus und Paulus', *Exegetica*, Tübingen: J. C. B. Mohr 1967 210–29.

Burton, E. de W., *The Epistle to the Galatians*, Edinburgh: T. & T. Clark 1921.

Caird, G. B., *A Commentary on the Revelation of St John the Divine*, London: A. & C. Black 1966.

——, *The Language and Imagery of the Bible*, London: Duckworth 1980.

Cardenal, Ernesto, *Das Evangelium der Bauern von Solentiname*, Gütersloh: Gerd Mohn 1979.

Charles, R. H., *A Critical and Exegetical Commentary on the Revelation of St John*, Edinburgh: T. & T. Clark 1920.

Chevallier, Max-Alain, *L'Exégèse du nouveau Testament*, Geneva: Labor et Fides 1985.

Childs, Brevard S., *The New Testament as Canon: An Introduction*, London: SCM 1984.

Close, A. J., 'Don Quixote and the "Intentionalist Fallacy"', in David Newton-De Molina (ed.), *On Literary Intention*, Edinburgh: Edinburgh UP 1976 174–93.

Conzelmann, Hans, *I Corinthians*, Philadelphia: Fortress Press 1975.

Craddock, Fred B ., *Preaching*, Nashville: Abingdon 1985.

Daiches, David, *A Study of Literature for Readers and Critics*, London: Andre Deutsch 1968.

——, *God and the Poets*, Oxford: Clarendon Press 1984.

Davies, W. D., *Invitation to the New Testament* New York: Doubleday and London: SPCK 1966.

de Saussure, Ferdinand, *Course in General Linguistics*, London: Collins, 1974.

Deissmann, A., *Light from the Ancient East*, London: Hodder & Stoughton 1910.

Didier, G., *Désintéressement du Chrétien*, Paris: Aubier 1955.

Dinkler, Erich, 'Bibelkritik II', in Kurt Galling *et al.* (eds), *RGG* third ed.; Tübingen: J. C. B. Mohr 1957, I, 1188–90.

Dodd, C. H., 'Some Problems of New Testament Translation', *ExpT*, 72 (1960–61), 268–74.

——, *The Apostolic Preaching and its Developments*, London: Hodder & Stoughton 1936.

——, *The Bible and the Greeks*, London: Hodder & Stoughton 1954.

——, *The Epistle of Paul to the Romans*, London: Hodder & Stoughton 1932.

——, *The Interpretation of the Fourth Gospel*, Cambridge: CUP 1953.

——, *The Parables of the Kingdom*, London: Nisbet 1935.

Donfried, K. P. (ed.), *The Romans Debate*, Minneapolis: Augsburg 1977.

Dormeyer, Detlev, *Die Bibel antwortet*, Munich/Göttingen: Pfeiffer/Vandenhoeck 1978.

Dunn, James D. G., 'Levels of Canonical Authority', *Horizons in Biblical Theology*, 4 (1982), 13–60.

Ebeling, Gerhard, 'Church History is the History of the Exposition of Scripture', *The Word of God and Tradition*, London: Collins 1968, 11–31.

——, *The Nature of Christian Faith*, London: Collins 1961.

——, *The Truth of the Gospel*, London: SCM Press 1985.

Farmer, H. H., *The Servant of the Word*, London: Nisbet 1941.

Farrer, Austin, *A Study in St Mark*, London: A. & C. Black 1951.

Fee, Gordon D., *New Testament Exegesis: A Primer for Students and Pastors*, Philadelphia: Westminster Press 1983.

Feuillet, A., 'La Dignité et le Rôle de la Femme', *NTS*, 21 (1975), 159–62.

Frei, H. W., *The Eclipse of Biblical Narrative*, New Haven and London: Yale University Press 1974.

Fuller, R. H., *The Use of the Bible in Preaching*, London: Bible Reading Fellowship 1981.

Gadamer, Hans-Georg, *Truth and Method*, London: Sheed & Ward 1979.

Gerhardsson, Birger, *The Good Samaritan – The Good Shepherd?*, Lund: Gleerup 1958.

Goetchius, Eugene van Ness, *The Language of the New Testament*, New York: Scribners 1967.

Gollancz, Victor, *My Dear Timothy*, London: Gollancz 1952.

Grelot, Pierre, 'Le père et ses deux fils: Luc XV, 11–32', *RB* 84 (1977), 326–47.

Griffin, Graeme, 'The colour of joy', in Nigel Watson (ed.), *Jesus Christ for Us*, Melbourne: Joint Board of Christian Education 1982, 55–60.

Hadfield, A. M., *An Introduction to Charles Williams*, London: Robert Hale 1959.

Hahn, F., 'Taufe und Rechtfertigung', in J. Friedrich *et al.* (eds), *Rechtfertigung*, Tübingen/Göttingen: Mohr/Vandenhoeck & Ruprecht 1976, 95–124.

Hill, David, 'Prophecy and Prophets in the Revelation of St John', *NTS*, 18 (1971–72), 401–18.

Hirsch, E. D. Jr., 'Objective Interpretation', in David Newton-De Molina (ed.), *On Literary Intention*, 26–54.

——, 'Three Dimensions of Hermeneutics', *On Literary Intention*, 194–209.

Hooker, Morna D., *The Message of Mark*, London: Epworth 1983.

Hough, Graham, 'An Eighth Type of Ambiguity', in David Newton-De Molina (ed.), *On Literary Intention*, 222–41.

Hunter, A. M., *The Parables Then and Now*, London: SCM Press 1971.

Iser, Wolfgang, *The Act of Reading*, Routledge & Kegan Paul 1978.

Jeremias, Joachim, *The Parables of Jesus*, London: SCM Press 1954.

——, *The Sermon on the Mount*, London: The Athlone Press 1961.

Kaiser, O. and Kümmel, W. G., *Exegetical Method*, New York: Seabury Press 1967.

Keck, Leander E., *The Bible in the Pulpit*, Nashville: Abingdon 1978.

Kermode, Frank, *The Genesis of Secrecy: On the Interpretation of Narrative*, Cambridge, Mass: Harvard University Press 1979.

Kiddle, Martin, *The Revelation of St John*, London: Hodder & Stoughton 1940.

Kissinger, Warren S., *The Parables of Jesus: A History of Interpretation and Bibliography*, Metuchen, NJ: Scarecrow and ATLA 1979.

Knox, John, *The Integrity of Preaching*, New York and Nashville: Abingdon 1957.

Knox, R. A., *On Englishing the Bible*, London: Sheed & Ward 1949.

Koch, Klaus, 'Is Daniel also among the Prophets?', *Interpretation*, 39 (1985), 117–30.

Kriener, Martin, *Aporien der politischen Predigt*, Munich: Kaiser 1974.

Kümmel, W. G., *The New Testament: The History of the Investigation of its Problems*, London: SCM Press 1963.

Lash, Nicholas, 'What Might Martyrdom Mean?' *Theology on the Way to Emmaus*, London: SCM Press 1986, 75–92.

Leavis, F. R., 'Literary Criticism and Philosophy: A Reply', *Scrutiny*, 6 (1937), 59–70.

Lentricchia, Frank, *After the New Criticism*, Chicago: University of Chicago Press 1980.

Lewis, C. S., *Of This and Other Worlds*, London: Collins 1982.

Link, Hannelore, *Rezeptionsforschung*, Stuttgart: Kohlhammer 1976.

Linnemann, E., *Parables of Jesus*, London: SPCK 1966.

Lüthi, Walter, *Das Lukasevangelium ausgelegt für die Gemeinde*, Basel: Friedrich Reinhardt, no date.

Luz, Ulrich, *Das Evangelium nach Matthäus*, Zürich, Einsiedeln, Köln/Neukirchen-Vluyn: Benziger/Neukirchener Verlag 1985.

——, 'Erwägungen zur sachgemässen Interpretation neutestamentlicher Texte', *Evangelische Theologie*, 42 (1982), 493–518.

——, 'Vom Sinn biblischer Texte', in Georg Pöhlmann (ed.), *Worin besteht der Sinn des Lebens?*, Gütersloh: Gerd Mohn 1985.

McFague, Sallie, *Speaking in Parables* London: SCM Press 1976. (In the American edition (Fortress Press) the author's name is given as Sallie McFague TeSelle.)

Maddox, R., *The Purpose of Luke–Acts*, Göttingen: Vandenhoeck & Ruprecht and T. & T. Clark 1982.

Malherbe, A. J., *Social Aspects of Early Christianity*, Philadelphia: Fortress Press 1983.

Malina, Bruce J., *The New Testament World: Insights from Cultural Anthropology*, London: SCM Press 1983.

Manning, Bernard Lord, *A Layman in the Ministry*, London: The Independent Press 1942.

Manson, T. W., *Ethics and the Gospel*, London: SCM Press 1960.

——, *On Paul and John*, London: SCM Press 1963.

Marxsen, Willi, 'Der Beitrag der wissenschaftlichen Exegese des Neuen Testaments für die Verkündigung', *Der Exeget als Theologe*, Gütersloh: Gerd Mohn 1968 52–74.

——, *Der erste Brief an die Thessalonicher*, Zürich: Theologischer Verlag 1979.

——, *Introduction to the New Testament*, Oxford: Basil Blackwell 1970.

Moody, Campbell N., *The Mind of the Early Converts*, London: Hodder & Stoughton 1920.

Moule, C. F. D., *The Birth of the New Testament*, London: A. & C. Black 1962.

Mounce, Robert H., *The Book of Revelation*, Grand Rapids: Eerdmanns 1977.

Mudge, Lewis S., 'Hermeneutical Circle', in Alan Richardson and John Bowden (eds.), *A New Dictionary of Christian Theology* London: SCM Press 1983, 249f.

Neill, Stephen, *The Interpretation of the New Testament 1861–1961*, London: OUP 1964.

Porteous, Norman W., 'Second Thoughts: The Present State of Old Testament Theology', *ExpT*, 75 (1963–64), 70–74.

Prickett, Stephen, *Words and the Word*, Cambridge: CUP 1986.

Redpath, Theodore, 'The Meaning of a Poem', in David Newton-De Molina (ed.), *On Literary Intention*, 14–25.

Rissi, M., *Time and History*, Richmond, Virginia: John Knox 1966.

Schweizer, Eduard, *Gott will zu Worte Kommen*, Munich: Kaiser 1978.

——, *Jesus*, London: SCM Press 1968.

——, *The Good News according to Matthew*, London: SPCK 1976.

——, *The Lord's Supper*, Philadelphia: Fortress 1967.

Snodgrass Klyne, *The Parable of the Wicked Tenants*, Tübingen: J. C. B. Mohr 1983.

Soulen, Richard N., *Handbook of Biblical Criticism*, Atlanta: John Knox second ed. 1981.

Stein, R. H., *An Introduction to the Parables of Jesus*, Philadelphia: Westminster Press 1981.

Strecker, G., 'Befreiung und Rechtfertigung', in J. Friedrich *et al.* (eds), *Rechtfertigung*, Tübingen/Göttingen: Mohr/Vandenhoeck & Ruprecht 1976, 479–508.

Stuart, Douglas K., *Old Testament Exegesis: A Primer for Students and Pastors*, Philadelphia: Westminster Press 1984.

Ten Boom, Corrie, *The Hiding Place*, London: Hodder & Stoughton 1972.

Theissen, Gerd, *The Social Setting of Pauline Christianity*, Edinburgh: T. & T. Clark 1982.

Thiselton, Anthony C., 'Reader–Response Hermeneutics, Action Models and the Parables of Jesus', in Lundin/Thiselton/Walhout, *The Responsibility of Hermeneutics*, Grand Rapids/Exeter: Eerdmans/Paternoster 1985, 107–13.

Tidball, Derek, *An Introduction to the Sociology of the New Testament*, Exeter: Paternoster 1983.

Vriezen, Th. C., *An Outline of Old Testament Theology*, Oxford: Blackwell, second ed. 1970.

——, *Die Erwählung Israels nach dem Alten Testament*, Zürich: Zwingli 1953.

Wardlaw, Don. M. (ed.), *Preaching Biblically*, Philadelphia: Westminster Press 1983.

Watson, George, 'The Literary Past', in David Newton-De Molina (ed.), *On Literary Intention*, 158–73.

Watson, Nigel M., ' "To make us rely not on ourselves but on God who raises the dead" – 2 Cor. 1,9b as the Heart of Paul's Theology', in U. Luz and H. Weder (eds), *Die Mitte des Neuen Testaments: Festschrift für Eduard Schweizer*, Göttingen: Vandenhoeck & Ruprecht 1983 384–98.

——, 'Willi Marxsen's Approach to Christology', *ExpT*, 97 (1985), 36–42.

Weder, Hans, *Die Gleichnisse Jesu als Metaphern*, Göttingen: Vandenhoeck & Ruprecht 1978.

——, 'Zum Problem einer christlichen Exegese', *NTS*, 27 (1980/81), 64–82.

Williams, Rowan, *Resurrection*, London: DLT 1982.

Wimsatt, W. K., 'Genesis: A Fallacy Revisited', in David Newton-De Molina (ed.), *On Literary Intention*, 116–38.

Wimsatt, W. K. and Beardsley, Monroe C., 'The Intentional Fallacy', *Sewanee Review*, LIV (1946), 468–88; reprinted in David Newton-De Molina (ed.), *On Literary Intention*, 1–13.

Wink, Walter, *Transforming Bible Study*, London: SCM Press 1981.

Ziesler, J. A., *The Meaning of Righteousness in Paul*, Cambridge: CUP 1972.

Index of Names

Index of Biblical References